SALES SUPERSTARS

★

HOW They Made It and WHAT They Can Teach YOU!

David C. Forward

PRIMA PUBLISHING

© 1995 by David C. Forward

PRIMA PUBLISHING and colophon are trademarks of Prima Communications, Inc.

Library of Congress Cataloging-in-Publication Data

Forward, David C., 1952-
    Sales superstars: how they made it and what they can teach you!
       p.   cm.
    Includes index.
    ISBN 0-7615-0023-5
    1. Selling—Case studies. 2. Sales personnel—United States—Case studies. 3. Success in business—United States—Case studies. I. Title.
    HF5438.25.F675 1995
    658.85—dc20   95-3859
                                                      CIP

95 96 97 98 99 AA 10 9 8 7 6 5 4 3 2 1
Printed in the United States of America

How to Order:
Single copies may be ordered from Prima Publishing, P.O. Box 1260BK, Rocklin, CA 95677; telephone (916) 632-4400. Quantity discounts are also available. On your letterhead, include information concerning the intended use of the books and the number of books you wish to purchase.

*To my son, David, who at the age of three
is the most persuasive salesperson I know,
and who teaches me every day to be
straight and honest, and never to promise
something I cannot deliver.*

Contents

Preface

It is time to play the word association game. Quickly, what are the first impressions that enter your mind when you hear the word "salesman?" OK, to be gender neutral, we will be using the term salesperson, but perhaps that is just as well. For many people the word salesman carries so many offensive images it seems that we really need a new word anyway. When you first hear the word, do adjectives such as pushy, aggressive, untrustworthy, and obnoxious come to mind? If you had to conjure up an image of a salesman, would you be influenced by such examples as the pathetic Willie Loman in *Death of a Salesman,* the slick, fast-talking Professor Henry Hill in *The Music Man,* or the devious hucksters in *Tin Men* and *Glengarry, Glen Ross?*

When I was a sales representative for Middle East Airlines, I would often have to make 13- to 20-hour flights to places such as Beirut, Cairo, and the Persian Gulf. I looked forward to those long opportunities for uninterrupted work during which I could write an entire marketing plan or create a lengthy presentation, unchallenged by telephones. Sometimes, however, the person sitting next to me decided the flight was a perfect setting to make friends with their seat mate, and he would chat on for hours.

Then a colleague passed on some advice. "When they first start talking to you, they will usually ask what you do," she said. "Turn to them, make your eyes light up, and say enthusiastically, 'I am a salesman, and I can hardly wait to share my products with you over the next twelve hours.' It works like a charm. They will excuse themselves to the rest room and never come back." That solution might have worked, but its implications were terrible. I *was* a salesman, and darned proud of it. I was not fast talking and have never sold a product or service that did not perfectly meet the needs I had identified from the customer. Furthermore, other than my faith, my integrity is my most treasured personal value, and most of my friends who are salespeople share the same traits.

When I fell victim to my employer's financial problems a few years ago, I was terrified of being unemployed in the midst of a recession. I jumped at a friend's suggestion that I become a salesperson for the southern New Jersey agency of a large life insurance company. I regretted the decision almost from the first day. For the first time in my life, I saw the actions of those stereotypical salespeople I described in the opening paragraph. From the agency manager to his sales managers and down to many salespeople themselves, they would scheme and plot new ways to talk members of the public into buying whole-life insurance, even when it was clearly not in the customer's interest to do so. They used abusive, derogatory language about clients and spent many an evening getting wasted at local bars. One salesman spent a substantial part of his day with women who had responded to his perverted classified ads in the newspaper, while his wife and children were at home. The agency manager made jokes about his behavior, never taking action against this person who was bringing in business.

While silently working at my desk one day, the sales manager and his recent recruit were chortling about an appointment the salesman had just made with an unsophisticated client. "That's great!" the sales manager yelled. "We'll go in there and rip out the cash value on the guy's old policy and use that cash to write a new one. We're both gonna make a bundle on this guy!" Of such unscrupulous, immoral behavior movies are made. When deceitful actions such as these are revealed, it forever sullies the reputations of thousands of decent, ethical salespeople. This event caused me to make two decisions. First, to get out of that agency that day and never return. Second, to write this book.

It would probably be a genuine bestseller if I were to fill the following pages with the actions of the disreputable few. That is not my intent. Instead, I want to tell the stories of some of the very best salespeople in the world. What kind of people are they? Not the person who got a big break and had a good year. Nor the son of the CEO who inherited the firm's most lucrative territory. What about the salespeople who are supremely successful, year after year, and are considered preeminent in their industry? They are superstars by any measure, and this book is the string of pearls that comprises their collective stories.

The reader can use this as a study guide for developing higher levels of sales success or can simply read the anecdotes as motivational fodder for their everyday inspiration. In his bestseller *The 7 Habits of Highly Effective People*, Dr. Stephen Covey talks about the need for a "paradigm shift." Salespeople whose paradigm—the way they see the world—still includes the foot-in-the-door, fast-talking, get-the-sale-at-any-cost approach of the past will never make the superstar list today. Salespeople trained a decade or more ago must change their paradigm for selling skills if they are to be effective in today's world.

Sales professionals can easily get confused with the material they find in bookstores. On the one hand there are many titles dedicated to one phase of the selling cycle, such as 101 easy closing techniques. Yet it is not realistic to expect that salespeople will memorize the entire book.

And what if their prospective clients do not respond precisely as the writer predicted they would? The other category of abundant titles is autobiographies, but how many salespeople who sell, say, sophisticated computer mainframes believe they can improve their selling skills by reading 25 chapters about a car salesperson?

Sales Superstars recognizes that different personalities and professions feel more comfortable with some selling styles than others. W. Clement Stone once said, "If you want to be successful, hang around successful people." Any salesperson could surely benefit from spending three or four hours with a supremely successful mentor who has discovered approaches, attitudes, and strategies that work.

This book is a mosaic of interviews designed to pass on this information. If you knew you were going to spend a morning with one of the top salespeople in the country, you would pepper him or her with questions. How do you find new business? How do you deal with discount competitors? How do you generate the enthusiasm to continue prospecting after so many people have turned you down? I did that for you. So if you sell real estate, for example, and have problems creating a target market, or sell something else and feel down when rejections come along in bunches, you will read how these successful salespeople overcome those obstacles. The industries and personalities covered defy a simple description.

Frank Pacetta at Xerox and Sid Friedman of Phoenix Home Life were both sent in to manage the worst offices in their companies nationwide. Both turned them around by setting the pace and motivating their salespeople to follow their lead and ended up running the top-selling offices in the United States. Phyllis Wolborsky sells $40 million a year in residential real estate in Raleigh, North Carolina, and tells how she still worries every day that her clients might not like something she does. Richard Kagan went from his New Jersey home to Los Angeles, too shy to even ask a young woman on a date, and entered the life insurance business. An oxymoron? An impossible predicament, a shy life insurance salesman? Read his chapter and see how he overcomes his reluctance to cold-call new prospective customers.

Speaking of shy, Irma Skaggs was so scared of even being around a group of people that she probably could have been diagnosed as paranoid. Yet after a lifetime of being a farmer's wife and mother, she decided to sell Avon to neighbors around her remote Iowa community. Today, at 69, she is one of the company's top producers. Despite excruciating pain and several operations that put her in a full body cast for 10 months, Irma sold $100,000 worth of Avon products from her hospital bed. Anyone who thinks they have an excuse for not performing because of a headache, a snowstorm, car trouble, or whatever, will surely take lessons, inspiration, and joy from the stories of these superstar salespeople and sales managers.

When I first started writing professionally, I learned the axiom, "Write with the reader in mind." The reader I have in mind is the sales professional who is perhaps having some mid-career problems. Maybe she is in a rut. Perhaps a former employer has downsized him from a management position and he can only find new job opportunities in sales, but is apprehensive about this new field.

I wrote this book for the new salespeople, fresh out of school and filled with enthusiasm—and a little intimidated by their colleagues who are bringing in much larger sales results than the neophyte. It is for the people who will never be in a future edition unless they change their attitudes and work ethics and make themselves more like the superstars they are about to meet. As one of the stars said, "I like to be the leader of the pack, otherwise the view never changes." I wrote this book for people whose sons and daughters and parents and friends are in sales, for them to see how one person can harness their God-given talents and solve enormous problems, devise creative solutions where everyone wins, build lifelong relationships, and make a great deal of money in the process.

As I went around the United States interviewing candidates in their high-rise executive suites and in Iowa corn-fields, I realized that I would be writing this book for them. I thank them for sharing their time, success stories, and innermost feelings with me. They restored my sense of pride in the selling profession. Without exception it was a privilege for me to work with a group of motivated, ethical, hard working, exciting Americans who are at the pinnacle of their careers. They shared their stories and ideas with me because they wanted to help someone else enjoy greater sales success. In turn, I have tried to write with the reader in mind. Now it is up to you.

Regardless of your educational level, race, industry, or age, if you can take one trait from each of these 19 superstars and apply it consistently in your territory, you will be one of the sales superstars I write about in the next edition. Good luck. Go make something good happen!

Acknowledgments

★

I wish to thank the following people, without whose suggestions and assistance I could never have completed *Sales Superstars*: Robert Alizart and Barbara Kracht of Airbus Industrie; Susan Chatlos and Karen Inman of Ameritech; Suzanne M. Bronski of Avon Products; Theodore Cunningham and Bob Williams of Chrysler; Glen Zimmerman of Digital Equipment Co.; Gerald J. Bauer of DuPont Company; Theresa Bolton, Holly Brown, and William Fraine of FedEx; Tom Rhoades of Ford; Dana L Fischetti and Phyllis Piano of General Electric; Tom Ensign of Million Dollar Round Table; Dan Jamison of Registered Representative magazine; Vicki Looney, Hal Rosenbluth, and Rich Yates of Rosenbluth International; Sandra Horner of Warner Lambert; and Tom Abbot and Phyllis Rinaldi of Xerox.

I also thank John Angove, Jack Edwards, Stella McCarthy, John W. Miller, Susan H. Rhoades, and Dave Twombly for their insight and advice. They epitomize all that is decent and honorable in the selling profession and I am proud to count them among my friends. Thanks to my wife, Chris; thanks also to Prima Publishing editors

Jennifer Basye Sander and Steven Martin for their patience, guidance, and expertise. Finally, I extend my profound thanks to the sales superstars whom you find on the following pages. I hope their enthusiasm, professionalism, and success are as inspirational to the reader as they are to the writer.

Allan Domb

★

America's Number One Realtor

The first thing one notices about Allan Domb is how much he is unlike the stereotypical real estate salesperson. He is soft-spoken and quietly self-confident. His non-aggressive attitude makes him seem more like a counselor than a Realtor; yet among the 1.8 million people selling real estate in the United States, Allan is the top-selling salesperson.

Allan Domb is an enigma in the real estate business. He is not working part-time, not earning "pin money" while his spouse is the real breadwinner, nor is he biding his time while looking for a "real job." His expertise in one specialized market is so great that he has essentially no competition. He is a self-made millionaire, yet his biggest thrill is selling someone a $48,000 efficiency, even though the sale barely earns him enough to buy a new suit. In an industry so highly competitive that the term "friendly competitor" is considered an oxymoron, Allan Domb shares his secrets of success with groups of Realtors across the country.

Allan Domb never intended for things to turn out this way. He remembers shopping for houses with his parents when he was a teenager. Although he was interested in real estate at that time, he felt he was on a fast track to a different career. After graduating from high school in Fort Lee, New Jersey, Allan attended American University in Washington, D.C. Throughout his college years he held a job at a lock company in Hyattsville, Maryland. When he graduated in 1977, he was promised ownership of the company's Philadelphia store if he would first manage it for one year. "That was my first lesson: that a verbal promise is worthless," he says, looking back on the three years during which he put his heart and soul into building the store's business.

At the end of the first year, the company gave various excuses as to why the sale of the store had to be delayed. Under Allan's management, the store's annual sales increased from $240,000 in 1977 to more than $600,000 in 1979, yet his salary remained at $16,000. By this time Allan was married and was unable to manage on that income. "I had to get a part-time job," he recalls. "It was a toss-up between working as a waiter or a real estate sales agent. I thought there was the potential to earn more money in real estate. That is how this all began."

Back to School

Allan heard about Philadelphia's Temple University Real Estate Institute, run by industry guru Jay Lamont, and he enrolled in the licensing course. His relationship with the school continues today, and he frequently returns as a guest lecturer, passing on his advice to aspiring Realtors.

His days as a student were long and exhausting. He was uncertain of his new profession, and he was filled with frustration as his doubts about ever assuming ownership of the lock company increased. His new part-time vocation had to be fit in around his hours in the lock store. He would be in the real estate office by 7:15 A.M., work until 8:45 A.M., and then dash over to open the lock store. During his lunch hour, Allan would make telephone calls and set up appointments from the real estate agency. Each

evening he would show property, schedule listing appointments, or work the telephones to build a real estate clientele. He rarely left for home before 9:30 P.M. "Those were *long* days," he admits, adding that he also worked all day Saturday and Sunday at his new profession.

As One Door Closes . . .

Allan had no intention of going into real estate full-time. Nevertheless, he worked hard at the business and in his first year handled $2.5 million in sales. Two years later his volume was $4.3 million and the year after that, $6.3 million. Working part-time, Allan became the top-selling real estate agent in Philadelphia.

"By 1982, I realized that the lock store promise was never going to be fulfilled," he says. "I had hung on there because the whole notion of selling real estate to someone and then having to start all over again looking for a new customer scared me. Although I was only earning $18,000 a year with the lock company, I liked the assurance that the check was there every week, regardless of my performance."

The realization that he would never own the lock store and the impending arrival of his son caused Allan to resign from the lock company and become a full-time real estate sales agent. "I joined the agency of Pauline Fuiman, one of the nicest people I've ever worked for," he says, noting that she became his friend and mentor. After her subsequent death, Allan opened his own office. In 1983, with one part-time secretary, he finally had a business to call his own.

Making a Commitment

Allan Domb realized early on that real estate is a profession, not a hobby. "Realtors have many choices in life," he says, "yet 99 percent of them do things they should never be doing. They waste time by doing things that they should pay others to do for them." Allan's favorite business quotation, which he attributes to John D. Rockefeller, is "The only difference between myself and everyone else is time and how I spend it."

Allan saw other agents grasping for any type of buyer and seller. "They would say, 'Oh you want to list a downtown condo, a farm 60 miles away in the country? Oh you want to lease commercial office space or buy a suburban detached home? Sure, I can do all that for you.' They cannot hope to give professional, reliable service and advice because they know little or nothing about the product." When he was a student at the Temple Real Estate Institute, Allan heard Jay Lamont urge the future Realtors to become "one street specialists." Glen Gardiner made the same case for specialization in his book *How I Sold a Million Dollars in Real Estate in One Year.* Allan Domb carried that book with him for three years. "Most people feel they have to go after the business," he maintains. "But if you are the best of all in a specialized area, people will seek you out."

Deciding on a Market

Allan decided to concentrate on selling and renting condominiums in center city Philadelphia. That was it! No gentrified townhouses, no commercial space, no tract homes in the suburbs. "If you found you needed open heart surgery, you would seek out the best, most expert heart surgeon in town," he reasons. "You would not go near the doctor who said, 'I do a little in pediatrics, some cataract surgery—last week I had a nice hemorrhoid case. I'm sure I could handle your heart operation,' would you?"

He devoted his first few years in real estate to becoming the leading authority on the Philadelphia condo market. He familiarized himself with every condo project in the city. He memorized floor plans, fees, taxes, and even the names of the doorkeepers. "If I know everything about that area," he says, "the most important components that result in a sale will be present: I will be more comfortable with the customer, and the customer will feel more comfortable with me."

Today, the amount of real estate information Allan retains is awesome. Nobody in the city of Philadelphia knows more about the high-rise condominium market than he. During a conversation he learned that this interviewer had once lived in the tony Dorchester building. His eyes sprang to life. "Oh really," he exclaimed. "Which unit?" When he heard the condo number, he instantly recalled the details of that unit. "Sure, 27th floor, facing south. A one-bedroom on the left, there's a kitchen on the right with a pass-through hatch to the dining area. Six hundred ten square feet. Spectacular views. Nice unit."

Dealing with Disappointment

Although Allan Domb handles more than 400 transactions every year, he can recall the tiniest details of any of his customers. His most difficult sale was a condominium he had sold for $125,000. Just five days before settlement he discovered that the authorities had placed liens of more than $600,000 on it. "My client, the seller, had never revealed any hint of his problems to me," Allan remembers. "It turns out the banks, the Feds, the IRS—everybody—wanted a piece of this guy. They even charged him under the RICO [Racketeer Influenced and Corrupt Organizations] Act." Five days later, Allan Domb brought the buyer and seller together and delivered a clear title at the closing.

Allan was able—through his skill, his network of contacts, or just very good luck—to bring that near disaster to a successful conclusion, but things do not always work out so well. Real estate professionals experience many disappointments: prospects change their minds, fail to disclose credit problems, or turn out to be perpetual "lookers." These disappointments are the biggest reason so many new agents quit the business in less than two years. So how does Allan Domb handle disappointment and rejection? "I think one definition of successful people is that they never dwell on failures," he says. "I have things occur every hour that some people might consider failures. But you need to lift yourself out of the mind-set of failure. It's an unproductive attitude to have. I don't care how big the deal might be that just fell apart, I give myself—at most—five minutes to think about it, then I need to get on toward a bigger goal."

When asked about his toughest lost sale, he ponders the question for a few moments, apparently at a loss. It seems that this time his storehouse of information has failed him. "I honestly do not know," he answers. "I don't care to remember them. I cannot even tell you what today's disappointments were."

Spreading the Word Every Day

Perhaps one reason Allan does not dwell on failures is that he is constantly expanding his network of potential customers. Having reached Allan's level of success, many other Realtors would feel they no longer needed to make cold calls. In 1992, Allan Domb set a personal goal of making 100 such calls a day, 60 of which must be made by noon. He still maintains that disciplined regimen. "I made 114 today," he says, looking down at a pad covered with tiny check marks. Allan Domb probably spends more time on the telephone than he does sleeping. He calls clients, attorneys, and prospects from his home, his car, and his office. He could be an advertisement for the telephone company. During one interview, he had a telephone in each ear and was able to maintain conversations with both callers simultaneously. In what must have been a momentary lull in the discourse, he looked at this startled interviewer and said, "Go ahead, what were you asking?"

His calls are brief, to the point, and non-aggressive. In many cases he is simply keeping in touch with a past client or a "bird dog" who has referred customers to him. "My business is to try and make as many people as possible know what I do and, when they do become clients, to ensure they are happy with my service," he says. Since he refuses to handle commercial or detached properties, his individual transactions are not large, and he relies on getting his name and expertise known to many people.

Building Relationships

When people first meet Allan Domb, it does not take them very long to realize that he is a different type of real estate agent. Long after the initial introduction, he continues to address his customers with formal salutations. The tri-fold laminated cards that Allan and his employees pass out to their customers and professional acquaintances state "We are Ladies and Gentlemen Serving Ladies and Gentle-men." They go on to list his "Three Steps of Service," a corporate credo, and on the reverse, 14 values and princi-ples called "The Allan Domb Real Estate Basics."

It is apparent that Allan does not see a customer as a means to a paycheck, but rather as a person with whom he wants to maintain a personal and professional relation-ship—forever. "My goal is to make every person I come in contact with more than a customer," he says. "I want to make them our ambassadors of goodwill for the rest of their lives." Clearly, Allan uses a long-term approach in building his business. "You have to," he says. "Too many agents meet people who might be able to refer them clients, or who might become customers themselves, and take the approach, 'What can I get from them right now?' It just doesn't work that way. My feeling is that if I treat this person right, give them respect, and gradually let them see how service-minded and customer-oriented I am, maybe they'll give me business in 25 years. That way, when the person refers a client to me in six months I'm 24½ years ahead of schedule."

From a Tiny Acorn . . .

Allan still remembers his first real estate sale. "It was to a lady named Carol Jackson. A nice two-bedroom, one-bath condo at the Academy House. There was a mirrored wall on the right side that reflected the view," he recalls. He has come a long way since then. Not only has he sold that first client subsequent homes, but he has also resold her original condominium several times.

As his business—and reputation—grew, Allan Domb was asked to share his knowledge with others. In addition to being a frequent guest lecturer at the Temple University Real Estate Institute, he makes many appearances nation-wide before groups of his peers. He has been active on the Philadelphia Board of Realtors. He has served as director, chairman of the education committee, and, in 1990, president of the 2,200-member organization. In 1990, the *Philadelphia Business Journal* named him Entrepreneur of the Year, citing "a career that has seen almost uninterrupted success."

There have been years when Allan Domb made 420 sales, and in 1993 his own personal sales topped $54.7 million. By 1994, that figure had grown to $63 million from the sale of 421 condos. There were no multimillion-dollar transactions to skew the figures; his average sale price was $149,643. He became the number one residential real estate salesperson in the United States simply by selling two homes a day. His philosophy? "Number one, build a business. Two, make a profit. And three, have fun doing the first two. Those are my three simple rules of business," he says.

Delegating the Administrative Load

Although he personally handles the customer during the listing or buying process, Allan has recruited a small team to assist in processing all of the paperwork that precedes settlement. This procedure sets him apart from most real estate agents, who allow the administrative burden to detract from their selling opportunities. "They should pay people to do those time-consuming chores for them," he asserts. "That frees the sales professional to spend more time with clients, more time bringing in business."

Allan's agency has a controller, a secretary, and a call coordinator/receptionist. He also employs a contracts manager to ensure that the minute, but vital, details are included in the legal paperwork, and both a full-time and a part-time licensed assistant whose own sales are not included in Allan's production. He owns a title company and a property management division, and has hired people to run them autonomously. "I'm the rainmaker," he declares. "Once I've sold the buyers their home or successfully negotiated an offer on one of my listings, I turn it all over to my support team, and they do a much better job for the customer than I ever could."

Excitement in Every Sale

Do the listing appointments or the visits with buyers still excite him? His face shows sudden animation as he answers.

> Oh yes! It still excites me, and I will tell you why. Sure, earning money is important, but you have to understand, a satisfied customer is *more* important. If you find the right home for a $50,000 buyer, and six months later they run into you on the street and say, "Oh, it's wonderful. We love our new home and I just love living here," that is worth more than money can buy. Realtors get very close to people for three or four months, and during that time they counsel these folks as they make the most important financial decision of their lives.

That feeling of responsibility provides the energy to sustain this human dynamo through 13-hour days and 75-hour weeks.

Allan Domb already has sales that increase by several million dollars each year. Where does such a sales superstar see himself in, say, 10 years? "I would like to be at the next level for me," he reflects. "That means buying a building that is prime for conversion to condos, then developing and selling the entire package. I might also be interested in doing the same thing I do well in Philadelphia, but in another city."

People can attribute success to luck, wealth, or connections. In Allan Domb's case, he has risen to the top of his field for a few very simple reasons. One is that he has a non-aggressive, respectful attitude. Another is that he is dedicated to the goal of calling 100 prospects—or people who can send him prospects—every day. Yet the two biggest reasons he has reached superstar status are that he has chosen to work in a specialized market, and he is dedicated to serving his customers, even though it means working painfully long hours.

> I had the work ethic instilled in me at an early age as I watched my parents run their embroidery business when I was a kid. I know I work hard and have long days, but that is the price you pay for being successful. Some of my competitors might say it's luck. But luck only comes to those who work. I still enjoy what I do every day. You have to if you are going to be any good at selling. When you lose the eye of the tiger in sales, or when an offer comes in on a listing and you say, "Oh, that can wait until tomorrow," that's when it's time to get out.

With that, Allan Domb is off to show buyers a beautiful two-bedroom condo on the 25th floor of a prestigious Rittenhouse Square high-rise. "It's just what you said you wanted," he tells the excited newlyweds. "Good security, neutral carpet, and a view from the balcony that will take your breath away." Allan Domb, Superstar Realtor. He is about to make not only another sale, but also another friend along the road to his place in the real estate history books.

Richard Kagan

★

Salesman to the Stars

Richard Kagan felt the call of Tinseltown even as a child. As a teen, he became a professional entertainer, supplementing his allowance by playing the piano. While attending Franklin and Marshall College in Lancaster, Pennsylvania, he worked after school as a pianist in a resort hotel. "I enjoyed meeting the professional entertainers who came to perform," he says, "yet I grew to hate playing the same stuff night after night."

He thought of himself as quite a good pianist until the day he heard the playing of another young man that had been paired with him to play at a girls' summer camp. "I realized right then that I was not even in the same category as this guy," he admits. Richard and the other pianist, Marvin Hamlisch, formed a deep friendship that continues today.

Broadway Bound

After graduation, Kagan served in the Army Reserve and was posted to Puerto Rico. "I went to see the show at one of the resort hotels," he remembers, "and I happened to run into the hypnotist who worked with me [at the resort hotel] back in Pennsylvania. We talked after the show, and he wanted to know what I would be doing when I finished my duty." The hypnotist described how difficult it was for

13

acts like his to get bookings, and how tiring it was to change hotels every few days. "That sparked the idea," Richard says. "Why not have a show in, say, New York, where the audience would come to him?" The performer loved the idea, and together they formed a plan. "I was only 22, and quite naive, but I had a lot of vision."

After he was out of the service, Richard and his hypnotist friend headed for New York. "We found an available Broadway theater, the Lyceum," he recalls, "and the show opened on May 19, 1969. It had wonderful reviews and terrific notices, but the audiences were tiny." Richard had not raised enough money to advertise the show effectively, and then, to make matters worse, an employee stole money. Just as the newspaper from his New Jersey home ran a story entitled "Hometown Boy Makes Good," the show closed its doors.

Richard wanted to get as far away as possible from the scene of his crushing disappointment. At the suggestion of some relatives, he moved to southern California to sell life insurance.

A Difficult Start

"I did not know a thing about life insurance," he admits. "I had no idea of what a life insurance career was. Although I didn't know anyone in California, I went out there because I was in debt and had to do something to bring in some money." Penniless, Richard Kagan began his new career on August 1, 1969. Looking back, he notes, "Eighty-eight percent of newcomers to our business fail in the first two years. It's a good thing I didn't know that at the time!"

His sales manager's idea of training was, "Ask everybody you meet—cab drivers, waitresses, bank tellers—to buy life insurance." This proved to be extremely difficult for Richard. "I was very shy and insecure," he admits. "I hated cold calling and was very bad at just walking up to

people and asking them things. Even socially I was shy. I could never go up to a pretty woman in a bar and introduce myself. I would figure out how to get the bartender to introduce us." As he analyzed his strengths and weaknesses, he realized that he needed the same assistance in his professional life that the bartenders were giving him in his social life. Kagan needed to mix with people who could introduce him to potential customers. He felt comfortable presenting the benefits and technical aspects of his products, but he just needed to find a way to get the introductions.

In Search of a Strategy

"I knew I needed to figure out a marketing strategy," he recalls. "The more I looked into it, the more I discovered that the people who needed lots of life insurance were those who were successful. The more prosperous they were, the more they had no clue about their life insurance needs. Very successful people rely on professional advisors—attorneys, accountants, business managers—to tell them what to do." While Richard was struggling to define his market, his agency manager was pressuring him to sell insurance policies. He was not interested in Richard's long-term marketing plan. He wanted policies sold to somebody—anybody—immediately. Uncertain and discouraged, Richard left the company.

Soon after, Richard met Sy Raboy, manager of the Connecticut Mutual Life Insurance Company's Los Angeles office. "I realized almost immediately that he was different," recalls Richard. "He encouraged me to plan for long-term success and helped me grow professionally every day. He even lent me the money to buy a new suit and paid my membership dues in a luncheon club where I could meet and entertain potential clients. When he walked into the office every day, he asked, 'What can I do to help you?' Never, 'What did you sell today?'"

Richard had become friends with the owner of a Midas Muffler service center. This owner organized a gathering of about 50 Midas owners and managers so that Richard could present his products. "They were all nice people," he remembers, "but we had nothing in common. I was there in a three-piece suit and manicured nails; they were in overalls with grease still on their hands. I'm not being judgmental, I'm just saying we had nothing in common and you cannot build a relationship in those circumstances."

Defining a Target Market

Richard realized he had to select a market with which he felt comfortable, and because of his experience in the entertainment field, entertainers seemed a logical choice. Unfortunately, however, he was in a strange city, and the only people he knew in the entertainment industry were 3,000 miles away.

Two weeks after he had begun working for Connecticut Mutual, Richard ran into some comedians whom he had known in his days at the Pennsylvania resort hotels. "I asked them if they wanted to buy life insurance and they laughed," he says. "Still, they really wanted to help me." After some thought, they suggested he become involved in a charity organization called the Thalians. "The members of the Thalians were all show business people, and Debbie Reynolds was president at the time. They were delighted at my offer to help them," Richard says. "Shortly after I joined, they had a charity picnic at the Playboy mansion. They needed volunteers and I was happy to help, particularly after I discovered I was the only young single male in the group!" He attended all the meetings, volunteered whenever they needed assistance at events, and became a popular and valued member. A year later, he was elected to the Thalians' board of directors.

The Big Break

"I was sitting by myself in a coffee shop one day, preparing for a board meeting," Richard remembers. "A man recognized me as a new board member and came over to introduce himself. When I told him I sold life insurance, he said, 'That's too bad.' It turns out he was an attorney, but he devoted most of his time to being the business manager for entertainers, although he would not tell me which ones. He gave me his card and told me to call him if he could help me with anything." Richard felt both skeptical and excited.

A short time later, Richard called his new acquaintance, saying that he would like to have the chance to bid the next time one of the business manager's clients had a life insurance need. The business manager agreed to contact him. Before long, he called Richard with the details of a large policy he was preparing for a client. "I have been using other life insurance people for years and I am very happy with them," he told Richard. "You've got one chance. Don't play any games with me. When you come in, you had better present your very best product." Nervous but excited, Richard Kagan had his first center-of-influence referral in his target market.

Kagan was thoroughly prepared when he met with the business manager. He thought the presentation went well, but the business manager was impassive, saying he would let Richard know his decision. Several days later Richard received the news that his proposal had been accepted. He was told to meet the business manager at his office the next week so that they could go to the client's home together. "Remember to look smart," the business manager warned. "If they don't like you, it reflects on me."

Richard went to Saks Fifth Avenue and bought the most beautiful suit he had ever seen. "It was really hip— for 1969," he says. "I still remember it: blue double-knit denim. When I arrived at the business manager's office, he took one look at me and told me to go home and change. Then he realized there was no time for that, so for the entire 45-minute drive to the client's house I heard about how offended he was, how I had really blown it. Then to make matters worse, we had a flat tire. Finally, we pulled up to a very nice home, and he still had not told me who his client was."

They rang the doorbell, and when the door opened, Richard Kagan was face-to-face with Karen Carpenter. Karen and her brother, Richard, were The Carpenters, one of America's top recording groups at the time. She escorted the two men into a room that had gold records covering the walls and introduced them to her mother, who complimented Richard on his new suit. "It sure is beautiful," the mother said. "I wish my son Richard would wear clothes like that. May I ask where you bought it?"

When Richard Kagan told her he had bought it at Saks, she declared that she would go there the next day.

"To establish rapport, we talked about music. We discovered that Richard Carpenter and I were the same age and both loved the piano," Richard recalls. "By the time I presented the figures they were barely paying attention. They had bought me 100 percent." He made the sale and had his first client in the entertainment industry. There would be many more.

The Same Rules Apply Today

Although Richard's first break came many years ago, salespeople today can learn from it. Here was a man filled with insecurity, entering a business completely new to him. He was in a city where he knew nobody, and he was uncomfortable making cold calls. On top of that, he was broke! Some salespeople go from door to door. Others use bulk mailings or telemarketing lists, hoping that a large pool of prospective customers will, by the law of averages, produce some sales. Richard Kagan chose a different path. After having identified a niche market in which he had no established ties, he decided to build a network by volunteering with the Thalians. He gained credibility by showing that he was not just out to make money, and influential people noticed how he gave his time to help their organization. Sure, he had some luck, but so do all salespeople who pay their dues with hard work and focused marketing. A salesperson in Idaho, Canada, or Florida, selling life insurance, real estate, or mutual funds, can follow the same target marketing strategy today. They can enjoy similar success in whatever their chosen niche might be.

Richard Kagan says, "Twenty-five years later, I do not do anything different. I still spend much of my time trying to find and cultivate relationships with advisors with whom I feel I can do business. Fortunately, I have built and maintained a very close rapport with the entertainment industry. I am extremely active with their charity work, to which I commit 25 percent of my time."

Getting and Keeping Clients

Richard Kagan provides life insurance and financial and estate planning not only to famous entertainers, but also to the owners and senior executives of several major corporations. "All of that comes from referrals by the accountants and attorneys with whom I have developed long-term relationships," he says. "You do not sell life insurance to the CEO of a Fortune 100 company by cold-calling."

Once he has established a connection with these centers of influence, he makes a point of getting together with them every few months to subtly remind them of what he does. "I have no monthly goals, no written business plan, no magic formulas," he admits. "I have had some terrible streaks where everything seems to go wrong. To shake off those demons, I go fishing or take quiet time to think, to dream." Although his commission income exceeds $1 million annually, Richard Kagan still admits to feelings of insecurity. "I am intensely competitive, yet I am always searching through my mind, questioning if I have done something wrong. I build strong relationships with my clients and their advisors. We frequently talk about very big numbers, so I don't know if all this mental checking and double-checking is really a bad thing."

One advantage that Richard Kagan has over many of his competitors is that he can deliver on large policies when they cannot. The average life insurance salesperson could not get a company to issue a $25 million policy on one person's life. Richard has devoted large amounts of time to developing relationships with the senior underwriters of several large insurance companies. They now accept him as a valued producer, one they can trust to be honest and ethical. "Underwriters are very serious, conservative people," he explains. "If you submit a $10 million life insurance application on a heavy metal rock star who just made head-lines for causing a fracas at a nightclub, he is not going to be welcomed as a good risk." As he reviews his career, Richard notes that he has sold billions of dollars of life insurance, yet has had less than $5 million in death claims.

His Biggest Sale

Richard's most lucrative sale came in 1977, when he met with two executives who were about to launch a television production company. They told him their biggest problem was coming up with an incentive large enough to attract top-flight talent from other firms. They did not have mil-lions in cash to dangle in front of their recruits, nor did they want to give away stock in their new company. Richard helped them solve their dilemma: "I designed a plan which allowed them to promise newcomers a bonus of three times their annual salary if they stayed with the new studio until they were 65. If they died before that, we would pay their entire bonus to their family as a death benefit. I put other guarantees and supplements into the plan, as well."

The two executives enthusiastically accepted Richard's proposal, and he has seen their vision become a 450-person multimillion-dollar entertainment company that is the larg-est producer of television shows in Hollywood. Richard adds, "The icing on the cake was that the owners ultimately got every penny of their investment in the plan back."

Dealing with Disappointment

Richard Kagan has not been without some low moments in his career. He tells about the time in 1993 when a per-son came to him for help:

> Another life insurance agent had mishandled him. It took a great deal of work and calling in of favors, but I finally got his contract rescinded and saved the client $300,000. For a

year he had come in here for meetings and advice. Then once I got him off the hook, he went to another agent who gave him a discount and bought the new policy from him. We got nothing—not even a "thank you." His only response was, "That's the nature of your business—too bad!"

Richard felt more hurt than angry after this incident, and he was disappointed that he had so misjudged the person's character. Over the years, there have been times when a series of personal or business setbacks has left him in a psychological slump. "All salespeople go through periods when they feel down," he reasons. "The only thing that works consistently to help me get rejuvenated is to go through my Rolodex and call my business contacts with whom I have a dear, friendly relationship. They not only give me a good hug, figuratively speaking, but I cannot tell you how often one of them has said, 'I'm so glad you called, I have been meaning to contact you. There is somebody I want you to meet,' and that leads to a new business opportunity. Then I'm out of the rut before I know it."

Building Relationships

Richard Kagan believes that the biggest thing that prevents good salespeople from becoming superstars is the tendency to sell commodities instead of relationships. He notes:

> That probably holds true in most industries. I have always noticed that car salespeople stress the commodity—the car— whereas they would enjoy significantly more success if they sold the relationship. It's the same way with most life insurance salespeople. They talk about policies, death benefits, and premiums. Customers don't care about, or understand, policy contracts. They do not think they are going to die in the foreseeable future, so the salesperson is never able to get through to them on their comfort level. The few really outstanding salespeople in our industry build relationships of

rapport and trust, then when they are proposing life insurance they make the benefits very visible and understandable.

Richard says that Ben Feldman, the preeminent salesperson in the life insurance field until his death in 1993, at the age of 81, understood these concepts. Richard shows the picture of the two of them that sits in a place of honor on his desk.

> We were great friends. He was my mentor—a legend. Yet when you met Ben you saw a small, portly man with a lisp. He came across as very non-threatening, and he would never talk about premiums and policies or death benefits. Instead he would say, "I am going to give you a way to guarantee your wife and children your salary for their lifetime—for just pennies." He was able to create vision, to uplift you, not by talking about death, but by discussing possibilities.

> He would say, "If you had a money machine in the basement that cranked out $100,000 every year, would you insure that machine in case something went wrong with it one day and it could no longer produce? Of course you would. Well, you are that machine. I need one percent to guarantee your family that it will go on producing $100,000 every year if you can no longer do so." You see, it makes so much sense and is so much less intimidating than discussing monthly premiums and your death. Really good salespeople always look beyond the commodity.

Richard looks puzzled when asked why so many guardians of the rich, famous, and powerful have referred their clients to him. After a moment he replies: "I believe the greatest asset I bring to them is total honesty. First, they need to be at a comfort level when dealing with me to know I'm working for them, that I'm on their team, and that my primary loyalty is not to some insurance company. Second, I am a firm believer in the principle that if the person does not need my product, even if they came to me asking for it, I have to be the first one to tell them they don't need it."

As an example, he recounts an incident that occurred at a lunch meeting earlier in the day with a 27-year-old man who had just made a small fortune by writing the screenplay for a hit movie. The client wanted to jump-start the retirement savings plan he had put off during the years he was building his career. "Let's start with $25,000 a year," he told Richard, reaching for his checkbook. Richard stopped him and insisted that the young man's tax advisor and attorney be consulted first. Surprised by this response, the young man asked Richard how he got paid. "I get paid when today's 27-year-old screenwriter acts with the help of his professional advisors who give him the green light," he answered. "I may not make the sale today, but I will never have someone six months from now ask the question, 'Why did I let myself get talked into doing that?'"

Enjoying the Rewards of Sales Success

Twenty-five years after his first tentative steps into the life insurance business, Richard Kagan is indeed a superstar. His offices overlook the Beverly Hills mansions and Hollywood studios where many of his celebrity clients live and work. His Rolodex contains the names of some of the most well-known names in the entertainment industry: Roseanne, Jackson Browne, Bill Cosby, and Cher, to name a few. He attends parties and private movie screenings at the homes of the stars, and his best friend, Marvin Hamlisch, took Richard with him when he was invited to dinner at the White House by President Reagan.

Remembering his early career aspirations, Kagan notes, "They told me that the ultimate measure of success in this business was to be the top-selling agent of a major life insurance company. That became my goal." He passed that mark long ago. He went on to qualify for the Million Dollar Round Table and is one of the fewer than 25 agents in the world who have attained the ultimate Top of the Table award in each of the 18 years since the award was established. Richard Kagan has addressed audiences of thousands, and Forbes magazine featured him in an article entitled "Doing Well and Loving It."

Richard Kagan became a sales superstar because he recognized his limitations and adjusted his career plan accordingly. Cold calling on complete strangers was something he feared, so he chose to target a specific market. He developed personal relationships through volunteer activities and cultivated an extensive center of influence referral network. Over time, his integrity and non-aggressive attitude became known among the professionals in his centers of influence, and they confidently sent their clients to him.

The Best Is Yet to Come

So what are Richard Kagan's goals now that he has met— and far exceeded—those he established in the beginning of his career? "The pursuit of happiness," he declares thoughtfully and firmly. "I am 48 now. I want to know: does my life make a difference? To my family, to my charities? I want to be the very best I can be in my chosen career. I do not want people to think that because of my achievements I have already accomplished my best work. This is a complicated business and there is a lot of competition. Nevertheless, I am still up to bat. I truly believe the best is yet to come."

Andrew Lanyi

★

From Minefield to Millionaire

It must be a movie script. The hero first escapes from a Nazi death march and then from his communist-ruled homeland. Penniless, he and his wife arrive in the United States. Knowing no English and possessing no marketable skills, the hero takes on a menial job. Through passion, hard work, and persistence, he rises to the top of his profession, earning more than a million dollars a year. He is featured in magazines, on radio, and on television. This chapter is not Stephen Spielberg's latest epic; it is the true-life story of a superstar named Andrew Lanyi.

Lanyi was born into a Jewish family in Hungary. In 1944, when he was 19, he was seized by the occupying Nazis and was sent to a labor camp. As he toiled to build a Luftwaffe airfield in central Hungary, he could hear the gunfire of the approaching Russian army. To escape the Russians, the Nazis forced the remaining 250 workers to march for days on end with little food or water. One night Andrew and his close friend forged travel documents, "authorized" them with a homemade rubber stamp, and escaped to his home in Budapest.

After arriving in his homeland, Lanyi had several close brushes with death when the Germans pulled spot checks on his hiding places. Soon the war was over, but the

27

Russians ruled his homeland. He entered university, graduated with a degree in philosophy, and became a stage director.

By the mid-fifties many Hungarians found their new political leaders to be more liberal than their predecessors, and many previously forbidden activities were now allowed. Then in 1956, the Soviet army entered Hungary, brutally suppressed the liberals, and imposed harsh military rule. Thousands were killed, many more were injured, and several of Lanyi's friends were taken prisoner. Andrew Lanyi knew he had to get out of Hungary.

He and his pregnant wife, Valery, joined with others trying to leave the country and began the long march to the Austrian border. As they entered a village near the frontier, Hungarian soldiers arrested them and held them in the barracks overnight. Again Andrew Lanyi found a way out. Under the cover of darkness he and Valery crawled across a minefield to Austria, where the penniless couple begged coins from the Austrian border guard to make a phone call. A month later they obtained refugee status in the United States and boarded an evacuation flight to New York.

Land of Opportunity

"Few people you will ever meet come from a poorer background than I," says Andrew Lanyi today. "I needed a job quickly. Yet when I got to New York, I found the demand for Hungarian stage directors very low—and the market for Hungarian philosophers was not any better." He obtained a menial position as a filing clerk with the *New York Times* that paid $64 a week, and he and his wife settled in a low-income housing complex in Harlem. On May 29, 1959, their son George was born. Lanyi knew he needed to supplement his income to support his growing family. "Each day I read the want ads," he recalls. "Every job said, 'Previous experience required.' Then I noticed an

ad for a part-time mutual fund salesman that specifically said, 'No experience needed.' I went for the interview."

Lanyi's thick Hungarian accent and scant knowledge of English did not sit well with the interviewer. "He asked me if there was any reason I could not handle the job, and I told him there were only three that I could think of," Andrew recalls. "First, I had never sold anything in my life. Second, I didn't know what a mutual fund was, and third, I couldn't speak English. Back then, mutual fund firms needed salespeople so badly that if you could move your lips they hired you." He enrolled in a training class and began learning about mutual funds. Although he was unable to understand much of what the teacher said, he passed the test. The next step was trying to find customers who could understand what he was saying.

A Salesman Is Born

Andrew Lanyi tried to fit into this culture that was so foreign to him, but it did not always go smoothly. He tells of one of his early experiences:

> I had been exposed to a little American history and geography back in my homeland, but I was completely in the dark about the way of life in this country. One day I entered a coffee shop for the first time. Noticing two other men at the counter, I sat next to them and figured I would follow their lead. A few minutes later, the waitress came over to the first man, and I could not catch what she said to him, but he replied, "Danish." She stopped in front of the next guy and he looked over the top of his newspaper and said, "English." Then she came to me. I told her, "Hungarian."

Knowing that his accent was a handicap, Andrew came up with an idea. He went to the New York Public Library and studied the telephone directory from Budapest, noting every name that was common enough to fill at least one full page. That gave him a list of the 110 most popular Hungarian surnames. He then went to the Manhattan phone book and began calling everyone with one of those names. He thought that since they were Hungarian, his terrible English would not bother them. Many of the people he contacted, however, were second- or third-generation Hungarians who did not speak his native language. Even so, his clever marketing strategy enabled him to reach enough prospects so that he was soon earning more in two or three hours of evening calls than he made at his full-time day job.

"In the beginning, every time I picked up the phone to try to sell I got a splitting headache," Lanyi recalls. After several months of ever-increasing sales, however, he decided to make selling mutual funds his primary vocation. He made appointments with nine brokerage firms and interviewed for a full-time sales position. During the interviews Lanyi said that he knew the firms paid recruits a stipend for three years while the new brokers built up their business. He also told them that if he was not self-sufficient in six months, he expected to be fired. Eight firms offered him a job. "When I started with Kidder Peabody, I realized I had an image problem," he admits. "The other brokers all looked Ivy League. I looked Iron Curtain." Andrew's clothing was not the only thing that set him apart from the other sales agents. They worked a typical day, from 9:30 to 4:30. Andrew, highly motivated to provide food and shelter for his family, started at 7:30 A.M. and worked until 9:00 P.M. He also worked most Saturdays.

Broadening His Horizons

Lanyi's sales began to grow, but his pace never slowed. One day his boss announced, "The research meeting is about to begin. Would everybody please come in, except Andrew, of course. He is only a mutual fund salesman."

Hearing that remark made Andrew so angry that he decided to become a full-service broker. "I started selling stocks, and within four years I was the top salesperson in an office of 40 experienced, well-connected brokers. There was no brilliance involved, I just worked a lot harder," he says. "By this time I was feeling more comfortable talking to non-Hungarian prospects. I became the top producer for two reasons: I put in more time than anyone else, and I listened to the advice everybody gave me and then considered whether doing the exact opposite might be more beneficial. Very often it was."

As an example of a piece of advice that he ignored, Lanyi says that one of the traditional "truths" passed on by sales managers to new brokerage recruits was that they should never waste their time trying to solicit business in the upscale neighborhoods such as Fifth Avenue, Sutton Place, and Beekman Place. The rationale was that the wealthy residents already had several stockbrokers, so the new brokers should concentrate on middle-class areas.

"I did bulk mailings to the upper-crust neighborhoods anyway," says Lanyi, "and my income quadrupled." He tells of his experience with a Sutton Place resident who had returned a reply card:

> I called him and he told me he was a lawyer. He liked my recommendation and bought 300 shares. I talked with him again each of the next two Mondays, and each time he bought 300 shares. One day I asked, "How come I can only reach you on Mondays?" He informed me that he was in Washington the rest of the week, so he gave me his direct number there. As time went on, I would call him two or three times a week, and he would usually buy my recommendations. I could not figure it out, though. He would always answer the telephone personally. Never a receptionist or secretary. I figured he must have inherited his money.
>
> Then on the day of President John Kennedy's inauguration, the guy came to see me for the first time. That is when I asked him, "What kind of lawyer are you?" He laughed and replied, "As of today, I guess I am a freelance corporate lawyer. You see, until yesterday, I was a cabinet secretary in the Eisenhower administration." Obviously, he did not want people knowing his private business so he had given me his private, direct phone number. I remember thinking, "What a country this is that an immigrant can make a customer out of a cabinet secretary through a two-and-a-half-cent postcard."

Time for a Change

By 1962, his second son, Paul, was born, and his client base had developed into a solid core of business. He had growing concerns, however, about the consistency and quality of his firm's research department as he watched the firm's stock recommendations of one month promptly decline the next. The declines were causing him embarrassment and were costing him customers. He carefully examined past research reports from eight other firms and looked at the historical stock prices of their suggested buys.

In October 1963, he joined Eastman Dillon, a brokerage firm with an outstanding staff of research analysts and a stellar performance record. Before long, Andrew Lanyi had become the top retail salesperson of the firm's 900 brokers. Being the top producer had its rewards. He remembers how, in 1965, it was unheard of for individual brokers to have a private office. He told his boss that since he spent more time at work than anyone else, and since he brought in more business than anyone else, he wanted to get out of the bullpen area. "When the boss told the national sales manager of my request," he recalls, "the sales manager was so afraid of losing me that he insisted I take his own big office, and he took my desk in the bullpen. The following day an interior decorator showed up and asked me how I wanted my new office to look."

In the 15 years that Andrew Lanyi worked at Eastman Dillon, he learned a great deal about sales and marketing. Sometimes he would slip into second place in sales, and occasionally he would not make the top 10. His English improved steadily, or so he thought. "Just as I felt that I was blending right in with Americans, someone would bring me down to earth. I remember the time when a client took my suggestion and bought a stock I was recommending. 'Now what did you call that company?' he asked me. I told him. 'What was that again?' he inquired. Again I repeated it. 'I'm sorry, say the company's name one more time.' I carefully enunciated the firm's name a third time. He ordered 5,000 shares of the $15 stock. I later discovered that after we finished our conversation, he had called my assistant and asked, 'What did I just tell Andy to buy me $75,000 of?'" Another client assured him, "You have a perfect accent. No trace of English!"

As investors became more sophisticated and the demand for top-flight analysts increased, other Wall Street firms lured away many of the company's best researchers. The quality of research on the small growth companies in which Andrew specialized deteriorated. "Most brokerage firms do not employ sales managers, as far as I am concerned," he says. "They are really just administrators whose goal is to motivate salespeople to push the firm's products. I have never advised a client to buy a stock just because the firm wanted me to recommend it."

It was a troubling time for Andrew Lanyi, and he says he saw the research departments of some of the best-known firms shoot for mediocrity—and not quite make it. New avenues of opportunity opened up for him, however. One day a highly respected, over-100-year-old investment banking firm approached him, and he agreed to join them. He started with a secretary and a telephone clerk, and his business went through the roof. Six months later they handed him new business cards. When he opened the box, he saw the title of senior vice president next to his name. "Then the firm let me do something never before conceived of on Wall Street," he recalls. "It let me hire my own research analyst. Why did I need my own analyst? Because in my opinion, their research department did a very poor job. I preferred to do, or direct, my own research."

A Firm of His Own

Five years later Lanyi was approached by the president of another old investment banking firm. The firm wanted him to head a new division, and they offered to handle the administrative work so that he could focus on what he loved most: research and sales. Andrew agreed, and the Lanyi Research Division of Ladenburg, Thalmann & Company was born. Within a year the division grew from 11 employees to 25.

Andrew Lanyi developed a new approach to research and came up with his own investment strategy. He believes that the two main risks to the company whose stock is purchased are that it will get hurt either by the competition or by a bad economy. His firm concentrates on looking for companies that have a monopoly or near monopoly. They also look for companies that are recession resistant or countercyclical, meaning that when the economy does poorly, they do well. His firm checks out more than 17,000 reports a year. They look for companies growing at 20 percent or more annually with reason to believe that that rate of growth will continue for several years. Finally, if the company can "cookie cutter" its success in additional locations he gets very excited. Lanyi discovers companies meeting these criteria before Wall Street does.

> As Walter Lippman once said, "What everybody knows, is not worth knowing." People come up to me all the time and ask things like, "Where do you think the market is going?" or "What P/E ratios do you feel comfortable with?" I don't care about those things. Market timing and charting are a form of witchcraft or mysticism. Sometimes they work. Sometimes they do not. In my experience, they generally do not. Furthermore, a P/E ratio is something any 10-year-old can figure out. Too easy. This is a knowledge business. You have to know more about that company than anybody else.
>
> I have worked 90 hours a week in this business for 37 years, and let me tell you what I believe are the key principles for successful investing. One, always buy the highest possible quality; two, buy the stock before the company becomes a household word; and three, as long as incoming orders are growing, refuse to sell.

Selling a Philosophy

Andrew Lanyi never wanted to be a stock jockey. When he talks with a client, he sells a philosophy and a strategy, not a product. When his prospects become clients, he always starts by buying them at least four of the companies that his firm has researched, never just one. "You see, the short-term market is totally illogical," he says, "and one company could go down in price. You can lose many customers in the short-term. When I recommend a stock, it is invariably with the long term in mind. I do so expecting my client's great-grandchildren to ultimately sell it."

As an example of this investment philosophy, he says that if you had invested $1 in H & R Block when they went public in 1962, your $1 today would be worth $1,050. A $1 investment in Automatic Data Processing (ADP) in 1961 would be worth $1,850 today.

He teaches his sales staff that if their passionate reasoning to a client does not persuade him to buy a stock they are recommending, they should politely let the matter drop. Although he knows that goes against everything Wall Street sales managers teach, he does not want to bully people.

"If the client says, 'I want to think about it and get back to you tomorrow,' we say, 'That's great. I hope you have a marvelous day; I'll talk with you tomorrow.' I never want a client to feel we pressured him into making an investment decision with which he is not comfortable. Remember, we are not selling a stock—we are selling a strategy. A long-term, meticulously researched approach with an impressive track record."

If there is one thing Andrew finds extremely disturbing, it is the shortsighted thinking of some clients. "At the very beginning of my career, I had a Hungarian customer whom another client referred," he explains. "I realized from the start that this was not an ideal customer, but he accepted my suggestion of a growth company with excellent long-term potential. He bought 100 shares at $50. Two weeks later he called me and I could hear the tears in his voice. 'It is 49½,' he screamed at me. 'I never imagined a good Hungarian would do such a terrible thing to another good Hungarian!' That was when I decided I was probably better off with American customers from then on."

Training Other Salespeople

This self-made sales superstar now trains others who share his drive, his work ethic, and his passion for selling a philosophy rather than a product. One of the first things he teaches is that working longer hours gives the salesperson immense quantitative and qualitative leverage in their productivity. As an example, he tells them that in an average day, to do their jobs properly, they will spend four hours reading research reports and doing administration. Assuming they take an hour for lunch, that leaves three hours in which they can sell. If they were to come in an hour earlier and stay an hour later, they would expand their selling opportunity time by more than 66 percent. He explains that if they were earning even $100,000 a year, which is much less than his salespeople make, that small additional time commitment would add $66,000 to their income. Andrew Lanyi rewards his associates handsomely for their long hours. Salespeople as young as 30 earn between $150,000 and $200,000 a year after their 18-month apprenticeship.

He considers "a high degree of natural intelligence, absolutely clean ethics, and the zeal and verbal ability to teach clients our investment strategy" to be the key ingredients he seeks in salespeople. He rarely hires a broker from another firm. His ideal candidate for a position would be a preacher, a young teacher, or a trial attorney. "Training someone from scratch is easier than trying to rid a person of their ingrained bad habits," he reasons.

One of Andrew's many anecdotes is of a salesman, a former evangelist, that he had worked with at one of the large firms. While the salesman was on the telephone one day, his voice grew louder. He rose from his chair, his expression becoming angry as his customer apparently was declining to buy the stock he was suggesting. "No?" he said, incredulously. "No? *No?*! They did not build this country on a 'No'! America was built on a '*Yes*'!" By this time his voice was at full volume and all work around him had completely stopped. As everyone in the office held their breath, the salesman's voice, calm once again, said, "Three thousand shares? OK, I'll take care of it. Thank you." Andrew recalls, "Everybody rose and gave him a standing ovation."

A Different Way of Developing Rapport

Although Andrew Lanyi is a very pleasant, likable fellow, he treats time management seriously and does not employ the techniques used by most other salespeople to develop rapport. He opens 95 percent of his new customers without having met them, and he still has never met 90 percent of his clients.

When he calls customers to suggest a purchase, he is aware of the high value of every minute of his time. He never chitchats about the weather or engages in small talk. He and his assistants work together to make calls as efficiently as possible. Each day they review the many calls to be made. When they are through, an assistant dials the first number and gets the customer on the telephone. Lanyi then picks up the conversation. Whenever he recommends a stock, Andrew asks the customer to take notes of the conversation. He will frequently pause during the talk to make sure his customer is really writing down the important details. His assistant remains on the line, making notes of the conversation and taking down any order the customer gives. As the call finishes, another assistant begins dialing the next client. When Lanyi transfers to the second call, his first assistant calls the order clerk with the first client's order. Then the entire cycle repeats.

He may not talk about the weather, but Andrew Lanyi is aware of the important personal details of each client. He sends a card and a small gift to every customer on their birthday, and he calls them personally on the big day to extend his greetings. He also sends cards at holidays and other special occasions. If, during a conversation, a client happens to mention that he is leaving to attend his daughter's violin recital, you can bet he will receive a card from Andrew the next day wishing the girl well. "People love to receive gifts," he says. "And everybody likes to feel appreciated. That is all I am doing."

Building His Customer Base

Although Lanyi's division has its own multimedia advertising campaign, the new customers that mean the most to him are the ones referred to him by existing clients. "Every year, at least two letters go to every client asking them to recommend our firm to new customers. If they make such a referral, both the new account and the referring customer receive a 50 percent discount on their commissions for the next six months."

As successful as he is, Andrew Lanyi still makes cold calls. He believes that no matter how successful a salesperson is, as soon as he or she stops prospecting, their business will go downhill. After 37 years, this sales superstar still spends half of every day talking to potential new customers.

What It Takes to Be a Good Salesperson

He has seen several really outstanding salespeople who turned out to be superb as brokers, but not as human beings. "They started working for their own pocketbooks and not for their clients'," he says. "That is a short-term view that amounts to pure greed and may end them up in jail—to say nothing of the many clients they might hurt. There is nothing wrong with long-term greed; there is everything wrong with short-term greed."

He notes that the New York Stock Exchange periodically conducts surveys to determine what it is that makes customers continue to do business with their brokers. He claims that the number-one response is always the same. Clients stay with their stockbrokers not because they are the best or smartest or most accurate stock picker, but because the client likes him or her. Andrew has switched firms three times in the last 37 years. Each time, he told only his best clients where he was going, yet the small investors found out where he had moved and insisted on following him.

Andrew Lanyi says the three most important characteristics for investment success are knowledge, discipline, and patience. He stresses that the last attribute is critical in the securities industry because during extreme market weakness, often the worst time to sell, many people bail out.

> Short-term moves reflect the madness of the crowd. In the long run, the price of the stock invariably follows the company's earnings trend. The overwhelming majority of brokers concentrate on buying. The art in this business is knowing when to sell and knowing when not to sell. If you work for your client and always do what benefits him, that strategy will bring you much future business. If you are selfish, you will keep losing your clients and will be starting from scratch every second year.

In his nearly four decades in the industry, Andrew Lanyi has seen many aspiring stockbrokers come and go. He believes that the biggest barrier to real success is their lack of determination and discipline. "Look at the other professionals who earn the same kind of money stockbrokers earn," he suggests. "Surgeons, scientists, top attorneys—they all invest many years in attaining their right to practice and then devote much more time honing their skills with the best in their business. Just as I fault customers for taking a short-term view of investing, so I can assure you that salespeople in this business with a short-term approach will surely fail. I consider myself the equivalent of a brain surgeon who specializes in only one square inch of the brain—but I have a tremendous amount of experience in that small area."

"Making It" in America

Andrew Lanyi delivers seminars on his investment approach throughout the country. "When I started doing seminars seven years ago, the attendance ranged from 7 to 20 people," he recalls. "Today I find between 400 and 1,200 when I enter the room. I can tell they have a hard time understanding me when I first open my mouth, but I lighten up the topic and make them laugh." Lanyi remembers a seminar in San Francisco when his accent so annoyed one man that he walked out in the middle of the presentation. As he left, he complained to Paul Lanyi, "I do not understand a bloody word he is saying." Andrew's son replied, "Don't be upset, I have known him for 30 years and I *still* don't understand a bloody word he is saying."

In an intensely aggressive, competitive industry known for its frequent disregard for ethics, the man who made it to the top is a slight, soft-spoken, ethical gentleman who has a deplorable accent and a passion for his approach to investing. Andrew Lanyi is a man who tells customers, "It is a commission I would rather not make," when they ask him to buy the hot stock someone whispered to them on the train that morning. He is a man so fanatical about time management that he says he fights for split seconds, yet he will spend an hour with a young recruit who has trouble grasping an investment concept. To salespeople on both sides of the Atlantic, Andrew Lanyi is a model. His story proves that whatever our financial, ethnic, or educational backgrounds, one can "make it" in America.

Thirty-eight years after he stepped onto the soil of this country, knowing barely a soul and speaking not a word of its language, Andrew Lanyi has made it. A multimillionaire, he owns a luxurious penthouse in midtown Manhattan and a summer home in fashionable Southampton. He is one of the top two retail producers in Wall Street history, and he frequently appears on radio and financial magazine features. His book, *Confessions of a Stockbroker,* is a success. With all the odds against him, Andrew Lanyi started out as a penniless refugee and became a sales superstar.

When he began, he knew nothing about selling and did not know a single person in this country to whom he might make his first sales. Any salesperson who offers excuses as to why they cannot sell should consider this man who did not even know the language. He overcame these barriers by working long hours, seeking creative avenues for selling opportunities, putting the client's interests before those of the firm's sales manager, and using the high ethical standards he carries with him as a core value. Today he manages his time fastidiously, and he still spends half of every day talking to potential new clients. For him, yesterday's victory is but a pleasant memory. He still pursues the gold ring he has set as the goal for today.

In the bustling streets of newly democratic Budapest, Andrew Lanyi must be the model for those who aspire to the capitalist dream. Now if we could just find someone with the right accent to play his part in the movie . . .

Marc McEver

America's Car Salesman

The average car salesperson sells about 100 cars annually. Those who far exceed that average become members of the "winners clubs" that are established by car manufacturers for their super-salespeople. Ford, for example, recognizes those who sell 300 cars a year as Grand Masters. For most car salespeople, membership in the "winners clubs" is the ultimate industry achievement. Then there is Marc McEver, the youthful, dynamic superstar who sells more than 1,000 cars and light trucks year after profitable year. He does it from a dealership not in New York or Los Angeles, but in rural Olathe, Kansas.

While in college, Marc got a job at Olathe Ford, which was co-owned by his best friend's father. He shuttled vehicles around the lot and brought them to and from the service bays. He also washed new cars before their delivery to the customers. "Initially, I just thought of it as a way to earn beer money," Marc admits. "Yet as time passed I found I really enjoyed the environment but wanted to go to the next level."

The Early Years

One Sunday afternoon he sat and talked with one of the owners about the possibility of moving into sales. "I saw how he got along so well with people and how he had never caused any trouble," recalls Olathe Ford's co-owner, Dee Bradley. "I told him he had to start at the bottom, driving people home from the service department, taking coffee to those who waited. I advised him he needed to put in many hours and must prove himself." Marc agreed, and the seeds for future sales success were sown.

Marc McEver still remembers his first car sale. It was on August 11, 1981—a conversion van. "I made $323 on that sale and was so ecstatic I took all my friends out to celebrate that night. I was in hog heaven and spent $500 on the party!" he remembers.

At the start of his sales probation period, he noticed that many other salespeople spent hours standing around drinking coffee. They would talk about the weather or sports—everything *but* subjects to further their careers. Unlike his peers, Marc would be in the service department, building rapport with the people who would, later in his career, often help him when he needed a customer serviced on the spot. Marc also built rapport with his customers. When one of them needed a ride home after they had dropped off their car for repair, Marc would drive them and would chat about their vehicle and the new models. It was easy for them to like this pleasant young man. The next time they needed to buy a car, they felt they had a friend at Olathe Ford.

During the early days of his career, Marc learned the values upon which his later success would be built. "We are big on honesty around here," he says. Apparently so, since honest is one of the first things anyone who deals with Marc—his bosses, co-workers, and customers—mentions when asked to describe him.

He also set goals for himself. The dealership's top salesperson was Curtis Walters, a man five years older than Marc. That first year, Marc set his sights on surpassing him in one of the subsequent 12 monthly selling periods. "You have to understand, Curtis was selling 15–20 cars a

month, in what was, at that time, a terrible market," he reflects. "There is no carry-over from one month to the next. So, no matter how well you do one month, on the first of the next month everybody starts again from scratch. We say, 'You go from hero to zero' on the first of every month." Nevertheless, in one of the months of his first year in sales, Marc achieved his goal of selling more cars than the dealership's top salesperson. He knew then that he was headed for a successful career.

Those early days had their lean times, Marc remembers. "Olathe is not a very big town. We were a rural dealership—heck, we had cows across the street until just a few years ago." With interest rates above 20 percent, he happened to pick one of the worst times in automobile history to start a sales career in that field. "Selling cars is not hard work in the manual sense, but you have to work hard at it. Those first years were very tough, mentally. If you worked all week and didn't sell any cars, getting up motivated the next day was tough." So how did he handle it? "You just had to keep at it and keep doing all the right things repeatedly."

Taking Responsibility for His Own Success

A giant tally board showed the sales of every salesperson in the dealership. When Marc walked past it, perhaps feeling down because he had not had a sale recently, seeing his name far down on the list motivated him to call his old leads again.

He had no formal sales training. "One day they sat me down to watch films; the next day I was on the floor selling," he says. "It was really a case of sink or swim." One thing this gregarious youngster had going for him, however, was that he knew a lot of people.

Marc made cold calls to get the prospects into the showroom. He was comfortable demonstrating how the vehicle met the prospects' needs, but he was uneasy about the close. He called on John Lee, the financing manager, for help in finalizing the sale. "I would give them the information on the car and quote them the price, but at first I had a problem getting them to make the buying decision," he recalls. "John was great. He would tell the prospect all about the payments, and they would buy. I learned so much from him." Without realizing it, Marc had discovered a strategy used by many sales superstars: If you are unfamiliar with a phase in the sales cycle, bring in help from someone whose expertise can move the sale to a conclusion.

Three years after his first sale, Marc McEver realized his job had become a career. "I really enjoyed it," he recalls. "I was Salesperson of the Month fairly often, and was neck and neck with Curtis Walters, who has since become the dealership's general sales manager. I was having fun, my presentations were really good, and I was earning decent money for my age."

He discovered, however, that while success pleases the boss and increases the paycheck, it can lead to resentment by one's colleagues. His decision not to join the other salespeople in idle talk while they waited for the next prospect to enter the showroom had made him somewhat of an outcast. One day, purely by accident, he dealt with a walk-in prospect out of turn. Marc was stunned by the reaction of his co-workers. "I took an ice cream cone in the face that day," he recalls. "I was upset that they thought I had done something unethical. It hurt so much that I cried when I got home." Marc's father was a longtime salesman and was Marc's mentor. When Marc asked him what to do about the incident at the dealership, his father's advice was, "Get your butt back in there and do not let somebody else ruin your day." It was one of the many times his counseling helped Marc develop his interpersonal and sales leadership skills.

Opportunity Knocks

By the age of 24, Marc McEver, through his ethics and his sales success, had earned the respect of his customers and of those with whom he worked. One day, the owners called him into their office and offered him the opportunity to run the fleet department. Two previous managers had failed to achieve even minimal success, and the principals told Marc they would back him with whatever clerical or administrative help he needed. "We knew he was young, but didn't consider our offer to have much risk because he displayed such maturity around his customers," says general manager Sam Mansker. "In fact, his customers just loved him. He was really sincere, hard working, and never gave BS to anyone." As always, Marc asked his "best friend," his dad, for advice. "He told me I had nothing to lose—that I had to try it," says Marc. "So I accepted. As it turned out, I didn't realize at the time just how great the opportunity really was."

Olathe Ford's owners envisioned their fleet department developing a foothold in the growing southern Kansas City suburbs by serving that area's multiple-vehicle businesses. Initially, Marc focused on the commercial market, with some success. The same qualities appreciated by his loyal retail customers—honesty, hard work, and dependability—also impressed commercial clients. Then he found a way to expand his horizons.

Envisioning New Opportunities

One day Marc McEver stumbled upon an opportunity that taught him to look beyond his local sales opportunities. As he was cleaning out his desk, he came across a company's brochure. In the picture on the front was a Ford light truck. Marc wondered if that company would buy their Ford trucks from him. "It took some imagination," he recalls, "but I thought that company might be an interesting prospect to go after, so I made a note to call them on Monday." That call ultimately led to his first true fleet sale. It turned out to be a very profitable cold call. "Last year, my sales to that niche were more than $5 million," he adds with a smile.

As that first fleet account grew, Marc noticed that very few of the vehicles they purchased were destined for the Kansas City area. That observation taught him to "think outside the box" and look for business where the buyers are, not where the end-users are. "I began to see our potential market area as vertical niches throughout the United States, but I also realized that we had no efficient method for going after those prospects," he says. "Then we hired a lady with extensive marketing and computer knowledge, and we could produce vehicle quotes in minutes, versus hours on the old typewriter." Marc admits that marketing was an entirely new concept to him. He says the expertise she brought to the department was a very big key to his success. Under Marc's management, the fleet department sales increased in the first year from 50 to 150 units.

Providing Better Service

The new technology allowed Marc to market Olathe's products to a much wider potential customer base. In talking with prospects around the country, it astounded Marc to learn that many of his competitors treated their customers poorly. "They acted as if they were the only dealers around," he marvels. "They would keep the customer waiting days for a quotation. They did not return phone calls. It was amazing." He established a policy of answering every request for a price quote within 24 hours, although typically he had a response in an hour or two. If a customer found it frustrating to do business with a dealer across the street, they now had one across the country who would quote a price, and sometimes deliver the vehicle, before their local salesperson returned their telephone call. Soon, companies around the United States were faxing their multiple-vehicle purchase orders to Olathe, Kansas, for fulfillment.

"Our department has grown an average of 25 percent a year for the last eight years," a proud Marc McEver says today. Their largest gain ever was in 1994, with Marc's personal sales exceeding 1,000 vehicles. Out of roughly 40,000 Ford salespeople, he says he has been in the top one percent for nine straight years. In recognition of this, Ford awarded him a Grand Master pin embedded with nine diamonds.

A few years ago, Ford changed the qualification criteria for the Grand Master Award. Now, in addition to meeting the sales requirement (300 for retail sales, 500 for fleet sales), salespeople must also excel at customer service.

Every customer is sent a questionnaire after their vehicle is delivered. "Good and Very Good are simply not good enough," says Marc. "Unless your customers give you, your service department, and the entire buying experience the top rating, you will not qualify for Grand Master, no matter how many units you sell."

At the 1994 awards banquet, Marc McEver learned his customers had rated him in the top tier of the three-level Quality Commitment program. "Marc is so sincere. With him, everything is up front," says Olathe Ford general manager Sam Mansker. "He spends whatever time it takes to be the best." The dealership's co-owner, Dee Bradley, agrees and credits Marc with the fleet department's stunning success. "It has done twice as much as anything I ever imagined, and that is entirely due to the honesty, hard work, and dependability of Marc."

Help along the Way

Marc McEver is proud of his accomplishments but is clearly a little uncomfortable with the accolades. "I'm not a really exciting person, I'm just consistent," he says. He admits that the many hours he has worked in the office have been at the expense of his personal life. "You don't get the time to make and enjoy many friends when you work 80 hours a week," he says. "I have gotten home so late and left so early the next morning that my wife Barbara has to check the laundry hamper to see if I was there." He considers time management to be the greatest obstacle he encounters every day, although he believes he is better at it now than he was a couple of years ago. "My wife is a very big part of my success," he says. "She is my coach and my partner. She is such a great mom that when I can't make it to an activity with 12-year-old Jeremy or 15-year-old Tiffany, I know she will. She lets me focus on the things I do best."

Marc is quick to give credit to the people who have helped him reach the successful position he enjoys today. "Dee Bradley taught me how to spot good employees. In a nutshell, his—and my—philosophy is: if they're honest and hard working, hire 'em." But he credits his dad, who passed away in 1989, with helping him the most. "He was always so supportive of me. He had such an abundance of common sense, I knew I could always go to him for an answer. If only he could see me now . . ."

Using a Direct Approach

If he *could* see his son now, Marc's father would behold a confident, personable sales superstar—one of the top car salespeople in the world. He would see a man respected by his peers and so trusted by his customers that roughly 25 percent of his purchase orders arrive with no price filled in. "I put the price on them because people know I can be trusted," he says. "They know I'm entitled to make some money on them, but they also know I won't take advantage of them, ever. I'll simply make a fair profit for a great job well done." After personally selling close to 9,000 vehicles, Marc has yet to have a client claim that the price was unfair.

How does Marc McEver get in the door of such large accounts? Selling a car to a local customer who walks into the showroom must be easy compared to selling one to a purchasing manager 2,000 miles away who has never heard of Olathe Ford. "Many salespeople won't ask for that type of business," he says. "They're intimidated by large accounts and feel more comfortable with small retail customers. I was too, at first. Then I got braver and realized there is no door too big for me to knock on. Today, I don't care whether you are the owner of a billion-dollar corporation or come by in a beat-up station wagon with five kids. I'll look you right in the eye and tell you exactly what I'm going to do for you. When my customers ask me to do something, they never have to wonder if I'll do it. They know once I say it'll get done, it's *done*."

Marc's no-nonsense, direct approach helped him when he lost his biggest account a couple of years ago. His client's company was bought by another firm and the president, with whom Marc had enjoyed a close relationship, was replaced by the new firm's president. Initially, the new executives used another source for their vehicles. Losing that customer cost Marc about $25,000 a year, but he stepped up his marketing campaign, and within a few months had more than made up for the lost revenue with new business from other customers.

The company started buying from Olathe Ford again, but created confusion by having several people calling in orders and changes, many of which were conflicting. After much thought, Marc made an appointment to see the new president, with whom he felt he had no rapport. He recalls:

> I don't really know what I had planned to say to him, but when I actually got in front of him, I guess you could say I firmly but respectfully blew up. I told him that I was sick of having five different people calling me from his company, each with different instructions. I said he just had to check with anyone in the company who had dealt with me before he came on board; they'd confirm that I only have to be asked once, and it's as good as done. I ended my tirade by telling him I wouldn't put up with this way of doing business anymore. I was fully prepared to lose the account completely.

To Marc's surprise, however, his speech had the opposite effect. Clearly, the president could not believe he was being taken to task by a car salesman, but he heard him out. "Then he said that he respected me for doing what I'd done, and that he agreed with everything I'd said. The meeting ended with him saying he was fully behind me in the way I wanted business conducted. I got back in my car and only then did I realize what I'd done!"

Marc McEver has never lost another account. "There have been bids where I might have lost an order because someone else quoted lower, but I don't want that business," he explains. "We work out the lowest possible rate we can offer and still make money. If it's strictly a numbers game, there will always be people lower—and higher—than us. I've lost bids by one dollar a vehicle, I've won bids by 11 cents."

Looking at Other Salespeople

In his 14 years in the automobile industry, Marc McEver has seen hundreds of salespeople in action, both good and bad. Some worked for the dealership, some worked directly for Ford, and others worked for the various vendors with whom he deals. He believes the biggest barrier separating the mediocre salespeople from the great ones is the work ethic. "They just don't put the effort into creating sales opportunities," he says. "Instead, they stand around the showroom door, gathered in bunches of six or seven salespeople, waiting for the next prospect to come in. You never see six or seven prospective customers walk in the door simultaneously, so why is that where 90 percent of the salespeople spend their time?" As Marc describes the situation, his frustration with his peers is clear. "They need to forget the chitchat circle, go to their desks, and get to work," he comments. "Make phone calls, go out and knock on doors, do a mailing campaign. Don't wait for someone to walk in, *make* something happen."

Building Relationships with Future Customers

Marc McEver has always believed in getting his name and service known by as many people as possible. Many of the customers he drove home from the service department in the early days of his career had just bought new cars. They would not be potential customers again for years, yet they liked his attitude and service so much that they frequently referred friends and family members to him.

The relationships that Marc built were not based on whether someone would be a customer in the immediate future, and because of that, those relationships would benefit him in the years to come. Many of the referrals he receives today are from those early days at the dealership. One long-standing customer flies in from Janesville, Wisconsin, to buy his cars from Marc. Why? "Because he knows he can trust me," Marc answers.

It Takes More Than Price

"Many salespeople think price is the key to more sales," he notes, the inference being that if a salesperson cuts the price, they will have all the business they want. "With large government bids, obviously price is their major criterion. But 90 percent of my transactions are not negotiated. The customers call me and ask, 'Marc, what's the price?' I calculate the absolute lowest rate I can offer and still make money, and that is the number."

It appears that Marc McEver has learned the secrets of selling cars and of keeping satisfied customers. In one of the most competitive industries on earth, his consistent average growth rate is 25 percent and he has buyers faxing him purchase orders with the price line left blank. "It's not a secret, or at least, it shouldn't be," he argues. "You just have to be willing to work for the customer. Too many salespeople are flat lazy. Take an extra five minutes and do the job right the first time. Be honest. Do what you promised you'd do. If you do all those things, you will succeed at whatever business you're in, because you've shown the customer that the value is higher than the price."

When asked how he manages to keep his customers so happy, Marc's answer is simple. "I just give the customers what they want," he says. "That's why it hurt when I lost that account for six months. It wasn't the money, I more than made that up from new orders. It was the fact that I had lost a customer. That really hurt me." What did he do to shift his focus back onto positive thoughts? "I just dug deeper into my core business and worked harder to please other accounts."

Those reading this chapter should know that this young man who dropped out of college to be a car salesman has people jostling to give credit to his professional and ethical accomplishments. Lynda Doane, materials manager for a customer who orders between 50 and 75 vehicles a year from Marc, recalls:

> He won our business away from a dealer we'd used for years, but he gave us much more than just a better price. He arranged a trip for our technical people to meet the engineers at Ford's Louisville plant. Marc did whatever was necessary to take care of his customers, and once he said he would do something, he did it. You never had to call and remind him. Marc is a man of enormous personal integrity; I could trust him in whatever he told me. He always went the extra mile, not because I asked, but because he sensed the need and volunteered.

The boss who saw something in the untamed wash boy over a decade ago agrees. "He's honest, dependable and will work for hours to help someone," he says. "Even the little things get taken care of. He returns every phone call, every time." Then, with amazement in his voice, the veteran dealer adds, "You know, I've seen customers wait two hours to talk to Marc. Now that is a testimonial."

For those who would say that the younger generation does not know the meaning of working hard to accomplish something in life, Marc McEver is the exception. Fortunately, for all concerned, Olathe Ford's management had the foresight to pick the youth to sell cars, then chose him again to be the 24-year-old manager of their new fleet department. Marc McEver has proven again and again that he will deliver. His long hours and dedication to building relationships with clients has earned him the loyalty of customers across the country. He has shown that core values such as honesty, courtesy, and dependability are more important than advanced degrees and discount prices. In an industry whose salespeople have traditionally been scorned, it is remarkable to hear his customers use adjectives like *honest, trustworthy,* and *reliable* to describe him. "I used to feel hurt by the car salesman jokes," Marc admits. "Now I don't even think about them. I feel a tremendous amount of pride because of the way I do my job. Maybe people don't realize that when we're first introduced, but I just pride myself on being one of the best."

David Koch

★

Federal Express Superstar

In the sales industry, many salespeople get into deep water and end up losing their jobs. David Koch, however, was in deep water when he landed his—literally. As a professional diver and fishing boat captain, he was deep below the ocean when the call came to invite him to join Federal Express. This lanky Bostonian who loves the sea says, "I told them I was happy where I was, and that I was not interested. Then a year later, they contacted me again." This time he agreed to go for the interview. As his next comment shows, David impresses everyone he meets and is able to make business decisions quickly. "They met me on a Tuesday, and I was on board with FedEx Friday."

David Koch says that he has always loved selling. "I was successful as a paper boy. I sold in a hardware store throughout high school, and worked my way through college, from which I graduated with a marine biology degree." When Boston's MacIsaac Office Supply Company, for whom he had handled inside accounts, put him on the road, he "blew away" the numbers on the accounts to which he was assigned. When Federal Express persuaded him to join the company's sales force for its new ZAPmail service in 1985, he thought he was on a fast track to a great career.

Unfortunately, ZAPmail was one of the decade's colossal corporate flops. Three weeks into David's training, the company canceled the entire program. "They put me on a six-month hiatus while the company sorted out the mess," he says. "Then in 1986, they asked me to become an account executive for Federal Express in the Boston South territory." He discovered a customer base that had a $15–20 million revenue stream and included several large accounts. For three years David Koch devoted himself to building that business.

Selling Based on His Customers' Needs

David Koch did not simply make sales calls to his clients. He learned everything possible about their business and showed his clients how FedEx could help them better serve their customers. Revenue from his territory rose dramatically.

In 1989, the company transferred him to California. It was considered a lateral move, but after three months, David was promoted to global sales executive. Now, instead of calling on law firms and midsized businesses, he was responsible for a few huge multinational accounts. Federal Express realized they had been viewing large companies such as Chevron, Apple Computer, and Bank of America solely as domestic customers who shipped both within the United States and overseas. By changing to a global perspective, they were able to negotiate contracts with the customers' international offices as well as their domestic ones.

David Koch was responsible for six global accounts in the Silicon Valley and San Francisco area. "I did very well," he admits. "My numbers went way up. A certain laid-back attitude prevails on the West Coast that I never picked up. So when I responded to customer calls and handled their problems and requests with a sense of urgency, they really liked that."

Building Global Relationships

As a global sales executive, David traveled far beyond the corporate headquarters of his clients. If a customer was having difficulty getting timely shipments from its Korean manufacturing site to its European distribution hub in Amsterdam, for example, David would be sent to both places to formulate a solution. "You cannot build an effective long-term relationship with a customer in, say, the UK by seeing him once a year," he reasons.

His work has taken him to Europe, Asia, Alaska, and South America. "My wife, Vanessa, virtually did not see me from Christmas until May," he says with a grimace. "Fortunately, she is also a Federal Express Hall of Famer, so our common pride in the company, and her own experience in what the job entails, helped enormously." Despite his absences while establishing his global account relationships, David Koch maintains that the priorities in his life are "family first, then FedEx, and me last." He says that balancing his time between building a superstar sales record and being home for every family occasion is difficult, particularly with a young family. "It is a thin line, and I have crossed it a few times," he admits.

In the less than 10 years that he has been with Federal Express, David Koch has earned the reputation for being the best person to send in to repair broken account relationships. "I don't know what the big deal is," he says. "I just go in and ask, 'What is the problem here? What do you need us to do?' Then I design a solution to meet their needs." It may seem simple to him, but when FedEx found that their biggest customer in the world—worth $70 million a year in revenue—was thinking of looking for another overnight delivery carrier, they sent in David Koch to save it. He is now part of a six-person focus team devoted full-time to serving that one account worldwide.

A Drive to Succeed

David seems to have an inner drive that compels him to be the very best. "I have always wanted to be number one at whatever I did, whether I was catching lobsters or selling office equipment," he reflects. "I set a personal goal really early in my career with Federal Express that I would be number one in sales with the company. The actual numbers do not motivate me as much as the competition among people. I still have that same goal."

David Koch's pursuit of new business is relentless, and he is most challenged and excited when he finds that a customer is using a competitor. This drive to find customers is why David Koch is the only person to ever attain the prestigious President's Club Award, Federal Express's highest sales accomplishment, for three consecutive years.

Although the numbers suggest that he is responsible for a huge chunk of his customers' business, David Koch downplays his own role, stressing that at Federal Express, the entire team is what makes the company successful. "They drum it into us from birth," he laughs. "I do not think I have ever attended a sales meeting that someone did not mention that 'People, Service, Profit, in that order, is our philosophy.'" With a service like overnight delivery, where timeliness is critical, the salesperson on the account must rely on his focus team colleagues to follow up on a customer call if he is away. They, in turn, rely on the van drivers, airport loaders, pilots, and customer service people to each do their part quickly and well. One employee with an uncaring attitude could cause the package from the CEO of a $70 million customer to be left behind.

Building Relationships with His Customers

David Koch often uses the term "relationship selling" when describing what he does, and it is what makes his customers feel like they are giving their business to a friend, not a billion-dollar corporate giant. That may sound corny, but how many IBM, AT&T, or Chase Manhattan salespeople do you know who give out their home telephone number on their business cards? David Koch does. He also carries a beeper with him 24 hours a day. "I tell my customers, 'If it is important enough for you to have to call my beeper at 2:00 A.M., then I know it is as critical to you as dialing 911. When that happens, I want to be able to come through for you.'" He reflects momentarily, then continues, "Look, maybe if you sell for someone else you feel you have to evade customers' calls. But I know this company and how it lives and dies on giving good service. So, to me, selling just gets down to core honesty. You have to be brutally honest. Even if you have bad news, give it to the customer. They'll find out anyway, but my way you can be proactive instead of reactive."

This sales superstar never had any formal sales training before he joined Federal Express. What does this truck driver's son do that makes him so successful, particularly in the hostile situations into which FedEx sends him? He answers:

> The first thing you must establish is trust. That is especially true with accounts I'm sent into where past problems need resolving. If the customer wants to vent, let them. You have to discover the root cause of their dissatisfaction, and you can only do that by listening, not by talking.
>
> You must earn the right to sell before you start selling, and to do that you have to fix the cause of their problem. Then I address the issues head-on. It is somewhat like walking right into a buzz saw. It can get ugly, but if something's gone wrong the best way to handle it is to acknowledge the ugly situation right up front. Then tell them how you are going to fix it, and do so.

Mistakes Salespeople Make

David has worked to keep many accounts from defecting and has seen the results of competitors' poor selling skills. This experience has given him definite ideas on good and bad sales practices. David says, "Of all the complaints I've heard about competitors, I think the most frequently voiced mistake—and dumbest for salespeople to make—is that they don't return phone calls. I've even called customers back from airplanes, and do you know what, they were still talking about that months down the road."

He sees overselling as one of the biggest barriers to sales success. Another is that too many salespeople don't think like the business to which they are trying to sell. "All they see is the small picture—overnight letters in our case—versus the entire scenario. For example, you need to have a mental picture of how the product comes in from Japan, how it gets to the end user, how returns or emergency parts are shipped," he says. "Too many salespeople talk too much. They need to spend more time listening, more time asking questions and learning their customer's needs."

Making Friends at the Top—and at the Bottom

When David Koch visits a company that is a customer of Federal Express, he often gets introduced to the senior management. He works hard to build strong relationships with the executives one frequently reads about in *Fortune* and the *Wall Street Journal*. Mark Spindler, a senior executive at one large West Coast account, says, "The thing that struck me about David Koch from the beginning was that he seemed to be our representative to Federal Express, not the other way around." He recalls having fought a battle with the local FedEx manager for over a year about a $23,000 discrepancy:

> We were extremely displeased with their inability to resolve the matter. Then David came in one day and, when apprised of the situation, told us, "I will take care of it." Within one week, he had resolved the affair. I discovered then that if David Koch says he is going to do something, he does it—every time. When you call him with a problem, he fixes it, even if it means he has to get people at FedEx's headquarters in Memphis on the phone and shake them up left and right. I have always felt he is looking out for us, and, of course, by taking that attitude, he benefits from the increased business we give him. He is the best FedEx representative I have had, period. Nobody else is even close. I cannot think of anyone who does it better.

David Koch does not build relationships with only top corporate executives. He also visits his customers' mailrooms and builds rapport with the shipping clerks and receptionists. That is where he is most likely to see a competitor's envelopes, or hear about missed pickups and late deliveries. He might have an executive upstairs hammering him for a 10 percent discount to meet a competitor's price, and then learn in the mailroom that the competitor's courier missed the customer's pickup twice last week.

Doing Whatever It Takes

Two incidents illustrate why his clients trust him to deliver, literally. "The CEO of one of my major California accounts called me one day when I happened to be in Boston," he recalls. "He had sent an air ticket for his kid to come home from college, which, by coincidence, was in the Boston area. Unfortunately, the ticket had not arrived, and her flight was the next day." David traced the envelope to Newark, New Jersey, flew down to pick it up, and delivered it personally to the student in Boston.

The second time was when he was still an account executive in Boston. He received a call at 3 P.M. from a customer who manufactured barcode equipment for the securities industry. "He said he'd had a recent problem with a FedEx delivery, and now he had such a critically important shipment that if it did not arrive in New York the next morning, a multimillion-dollar deal would be blown." David assured the executive that the company would deliver the package on time. After he hung up, however, he began thinking of all the things that could go wrong that were out of his control: bad weather, an aircraft mechanical delay, an accident. So he drove to the customer's office, loaded the package into his Jeep, and made the 450-mile round-trip himself. Not only did he earn the permanent gratitude of his client, but five years later that company merged with another and became a Federal Express global account.

Setting and Measuring Performance Goals

David Koch sets goals and measures his progress toward them daily. "Federal Express sets us targets for each territory, and our quarterly bonus is predicated on making those numbers," he explains. "Nevertheless, I set my personal goals much higher than the company's. Typically, they might set a goal at 8 percent above last year's results, whereas I will shoot for an increase of between 20 and 100 percent. I have made my bonus every quarter for eight years. I've never missed. My rule is, the first quarter I miss making my sales bonus will be my last quarter with FedEx."

David Koch is serious about achieving his goals. He always writes them down, divided into daily increments. "You cannot see what a $3-million-a-year account is," he says. "So break it down by the number of annual work days and the average package rate. Then it is really easy to see that this account needs to be shipping, say, 15 packages a day, and you eyeball how they are doing."

Some salespeople rely on motivational books and tapes to keep their outlook positive. David finds most of them "corny," and he very rarely finds himself in poor spirits, anyway. If he does need a morale boost, he says the best motivator he ever knew is Bill Razzouk, FedEx's Executive Vice President of Worldwide Customer Operations. "If you consider me a sales superstar, then he is the poster boy of sales superstars," he says. "Bill is really a quality, commonsense guy who still uses the best business selling skills I have ever seen, every day." David Koch has a track record of beating challenging goals and has the satisfaction of being sent by his company to save their best accounts. It is understandable why he never worries about ruts or job security.

The Rewards of Cold-Calling

Many salespeople are reluctant to make sales calls and especially fear face-to-face cold calls. David sees it differently:

"Much of my success at Federal Express has come because I always made that extra cold call," he claims. He tells of the time when, at the end of a long, tiring day he was about to drive home after cold-calling in a Massachusetts industrial park. As exhausted as he was, he forced himself to call on one more firm. "Thank God you are here," the receptionist said when he introduced himself. "Emery has failed to show up for two days in a row and we have all these urgent shipments that have to get out." David went right to his car, returned with a box of air bills, and wrote them all up for his large new customer. "I still have that account five years later," he adds.

And the Winner Is . . .

Incidents like this are the reason that David Koch is the first three-time winner of Federal Express's President's Club Award, an award received by only the few salespeople who attain a certain sales level each year. In 1994, while attending the firm's Global Sales Rally in Las Vegas, David Koch was "absolutely stunned" to hear the announcement that they were inducting him into the Federal Express Hall of Fame, an honor bestowed annually upon perhaps 30 of the company's 100,000 employees. "It was the best high I have ever had!" he exclaims. "It was just like the Academy Awards, sitting there with thousands of people and hearing that they had honored me with such recognition."

Almost before the applause had died down, however, David Koch was back on the phone and in his customers' offices, strengthening his relationships. "You are only as good as you were yesterday, so don't sit on your laurels," he warns. "Surfers might think that riding the wave is easy, but even the biggest wave always dies. Between us, UPS, and Airborne Express, it is like war out there, and I do not intend to lose a single battle."

It has been almost 10 years since this New England lobsterman became a Federal Express salesman. By all accounts, both the company and David Koch made the right choice. His skills have added millions of dollars to the firm's revenues, and David Koch is very proud of the company he represents.

The Pride Shows Through

When asked to tell "a little about himself" during the initial interview for this chapter, David spent the first 10 minutes extolling the virtues of Federal Express from an employee's perspective. "This company really takes care of its people," he says. "They have a no-layoff policy, and they pour tons of recognition on staff who perform. It is a very, very good company for which to work."

He told of the time when he rushed his pregnant wife to the hospital where she delivered twins two months prematurely. The tiny babies were in critical condition for weeks while the medical staff worked to gradually build up their weight and immune systems. "For two months, my boss told me the company did not even want to hear from me," says David. "FedEx basically said, 'Forget about your customers, we will take care of them. You take care of your family.' This company bought real loyalty from me in the way they treated my family when we had a crisis."

For David, going the extra mile works both ways. Some time after the birth of the twins, David noticed a Federal Express van on the side of a country road. He pulled over and discovered the vehicle had broken down. To avoid late delivery of customer packages, he transferred everything to his own car, then dropped it all off at the FedEx depot for final distribution on another van. It is hard to know who deserves the greater credit: FedEx for instilling their team approach philosophy into their employees, or David Koch for having the initiative to pull over and help the delivery van driver.

Even without that example, however, it is easy to see why David Koch has become a superstar. He excels at his job because he *believes* in what he is selling. His love of selling keeps him alert for opportunities long after average salespeople have put their minds into quit mode for the day. His daily goals keep him abreast of his progress, and as the examples in this chapter show, he is willing to go far beyond the call of duty to accommodate a customer's special request. Perhaps the greatest difference between the underachieving salesperson and David Koch is that David feels he has to earn the right to sell by listening to the client, not talking to them.

He reveals that a major competitor recently dangled a six-figure carrot in front of him to try to get him to jump ship, but he told them he was not interested. "With Federal Express you always have the feeling the company is on the edge of some innovation that will improve our service or fill a niche even better. I have the feeling that if I left, I would go through life disappointed with that decision. I just cannot imagine selling for a company that was not number one. Federal Express truly is the best at what they do. That is what drives me to give my absolute best to every customer every single day."

Phyllis Wolborsky

★

Real Estate's
$40 Million Woman

Sitting in the office of Phyllis Wolborsky, you can see that she is a superstar even before you meet her. Plaques, awards, and framed press articles cover almost every square inch of wall space, proof of her place at the pinnacle of her profession. A large glass display case shows off the trophies and medallions she has received over the years. The case also contains photographs of Phyllis receiving top awards throughout her 25-year career. In this office, the desk, which most people use to arrange their work, is covered by the 30 two-foot-tall obelisks she has received for sales achievements. As the visitor stands in awe at this scene, in walks the superstar. Fasten your seat belts. You are about to meet Phyllis Wolborsky.

It was not supposed to be this way, she says, recalling that although she had sold encyclopedias and novelties since the age of 14, she entered the workforce as a book-keeper. She grew up in Atlanta and married in 1966. The following year, she and her husband, Bernie, moved to Raleigh, North Carolina, where Bernie had found a better job. "Never in a million years would I have thought of myself as becoming someone special," she says.

After several months in their Raleigh apartment, quarters that became cramped when their son Brad was born, the Wolborskys decided to build a new home. Bernie's job required that he travel much of the time, so it fell to Phyllis to make the arrangements for their new house. She spent countless days taking Brad through different neighborhoods in a stroller, noting the house styles and characteristics that appealed to her. When the time came to select the lot and work with a builder, Phyllis knew exactly what she wanted in their new home.

She became so knowledgeable about what to look for in a house that many of their new friends in town began calling Phyllis for advice on what they should look for as they bought their first homes. After having spent more than a year dispensing free advice as the city's premier unpaid real estate authority, she was convinced by her friend, Elaine Sandman, to get her real estate license. "The two of us took the course together," Phyllis says. "I passed the exam by just one point. That is how close I came to staying a housewife." Phyllis thought she would not use her new ability for a while, but Elaine talked her into entering the business as partners, and together they launched a career.

"I still remember everything about my first sale," she recalls. "I can even remember exactly what I was wearing when my first commission check arrived. I went tearing home to Bernie and told him, 'I had so much fun working with this buyer. They are so happy I found them the perfect home, and look, I got paid $400 for it!'"

A Fast Start to a New Career

Those early days were not easy for Phyllis and Elaine. "Other Realtors told us, 'This is a man's business. The five female Realtors in Raleigh are our limit,'" she remembers. "Nevertheless, a new, more confident me was awakening. I even dressed differently than the other sales ladies, eschewing the conservative navy blazers and gray wool skirts that they favored." It didn't take the real estate profession in

this sleepy southern city long to begin taking note of the sales generated by this dynamic duo.

"In our first six months in the business, we did $1.4 million in sales," says Phyllis. "And in 1969, that wasn't hay!" Year after year, the two friends talked real estate in the office, rode together to every appointment, and then talked from their homes by telephone long into the evening. With each passing year, their business saw explosive growth. In 1982, a year in which the two women generated $8 million in sales, Elaine retired.

Going Solo

For many salespeople, losing such a trusted resource and valuable co-worker would have meant a subsequent drop in sales. Phyllis Wolborsky, however, was determined to take her practice to new heights. The next year, on her own, she produced $14 million in real estate sales, and the *Raleigh Times* ran a front-page feature headlined "The $14 Million Woman." Despite her success, Phyllis has always managed to balance her mounting responsibilities at home—at one point having four children, including twins, under the age of six—with the steady growth of her business.

Today Phyllis Wolborsky is one of the top producing Realtors in the nation. What is remarkable is that she attains such eminence not by selling million-dollar Beverly Hills mansions, but by selling homes in suburban Raleigh that have an average price of $212,000. The firm where she works, Howard, Perry and Walston, is affiliated with the Better Homes and Gardens network, and Phyllis has qualified for their nationwide President's Council Top Producer Award each year for the past 12 years.

What has motivated such consistent achievement? "I came from a very loving family," she says quietly, "but there was never a morning that I didn't wake up as a little girl to hear my parents arguing about money. That was really the only thing I ever heard them argue about. I know my dad did his best for us, but I swore to myself never to let that happen with my family. Today, I have four sons that I adore, but we never discuss money. They have no idea what I make, and I will not allow money to be the ruler. They have each had to work every summer so that they will appreciate the value of money. So I guess in the early days when I saw I could earn a lot of money doing what I loved, and I saw that it was something that would help put my family on a firm financial foundation, that is what motivated me."

Don't Chase Just the Big Ones

Despite her consistently high sales numbers, Phyllis does not have to think long to recall her most lucrative sale. "I had a $600,000 sale once, but only once!" she says. "You see, we don't have million-dollar homes around here. Somebody could waste a year trying to get a $600,000 sale. I'd rather sell a customer a $150,000 home and take such good care of her that she will refer three friends to me who will each buy $150,000 houses." She chuckles about how she hears, through the industry grapevine, what jealous competitors say about her. "They think I am crazy," she says, "because I work with first-time home buyers. Maybe *they* think they're a waste of time, but that's because they don't qualify the customer first." Her back straightens and her face becomes flushed as she says with conviction, "I do not believe you should ever limit yourself. You see, my first-time home buyers know other first-time buyers. My first-time home buyers will, in a few years, become first-time home *sellers* and second-time home buyers."

Phyllis tells how some of the nation's top real estate producers shun buyers because of the time it takes to drive them around and the uncertainties that come with their mortgage applications. They prefer sellers because a seller is contracted with the broker, no matter who ultimately finds the buyer. She considers herself in the relationship-building business and is happy to work either side of the transaction. In 1994, her business was evenly split between homes bought and listings sold; she had 79 of each.

The affable Wolborsky recognizes that her genial personality does not fit every prospective client. "We deal with many high tech and scientific types here in the Research Triangle area," she explains. "You have to be able to quickly read a person's personality type and adjust your style to that person. Otherwise, you are never going to make the connection."

Stick to What You Know

Phyllis claims the biggest mistake she ever made was in diverting from her area of expertise. She let herself be talked into making an audio cassette series on her industry success, the plan being to market them to Realtors around the country who wanted to learn from her achievements. After her basement was filled with the tapes, she suddenly realized she had neither the time nor the ability to sell them. "I do one thing and I do it well—listing and selling homes. Now I know to stick to that," she says. The same rule applies to business opportunities outside her focused market area. "If I get a commercial client or someone wanting a property on the other side of town, I refer them out to a specialist in that area. Why be greedy? It is just not fair of me to handle something with which I have no expertise."

If Phyllis Wolborsky lacks the skills to market instructional tapes, she certainly knows her stuff when it comes to promoting her real estate practice. All of her advertising, from business cards to highway billboards, includes her picture. The message she continually drives home is her consistent sales accomplishments. One powerful brochure states, "The average real estate agent sold three homes last year. Phyllis Wolborsky sold that many yesterday." Between her advertising, her thousands of past customers, and the press attention she receives, Phyllis is a celebrity around town. "People come up to me all the time and strike up conversations out of the blue," she laughs. "Sometimes they will want my opinion on mortgage rates. Others will just want to chat. 'I guess you must be Mr. Phyllis' they say if Bernie is with me." Sometimes she is not so pleased at the interruption. "I have had a person come up to me in a restaurant and say, 'How can you go out to dinner when my house still has not sold yet?'" she grimaces.

She realizes that not every customer will always be happy with her all the time, yet her passion to please drives her through 70-hour work weeks. "People know me. They trust me. They know I am a people pleaser. Still, at 52 years of age, I worry every day that I might make someone unhappy," she admits. "I went to my doctor and confessed to being a workaholic, and he said, 'Is that so bad? Your competitors and co-workers with whom you don't go out to lunch every day might think so. But you take care of your health, you pamper your customers, and you take time with your family. So what is so bad about being a workaholic?'"

Communicating with Clients

When Phyllis visits a prospect's home on a listing appointment, she tells them up front what they can expect from her. She discusses pricing, advertising, home improvements, and open houses. "Ultimately, I have to be in charge of the way it is done," she adds. "If the chemistry, price, or needed renovations are not mutually agreeable, I'll walk out. I do not want my sale sign sitting on their property getting stale. If they will not heed my advice, there is no need to pay for it." Wolborsky walks away from 80–90 percent of these appointments with a signed listing agreement.

She communicates with the client frequently, passing on feedback from prospective buyers and from other agents who have toured the property. With dozens of homes listed simultaneously, this can be quite a challenge. According to Phyllis, poor communication between the listing agent and the homeowner is one of the primary reasons homeowners do not re-sign with a broker when the listing contract expires. "I cannot call them every day, but they definitely hear from me the minute anything significant occurs," Phyllis points out.

Some Still Get Away

Even with all of her marketing and sales success, there are some opportunities that go to her competitors. If the client goes with an agent who suggests that a much higher listing price is appropriate, Phyllis shrugs it off. "They can *list* the house as high as they want, but I know it'll never sell for that," she says. "So I will go back in 180 days, when the first listing expires, and then the seller is really motivated."

Occasionally, she loses a listing to what she calls commission gypsies—agents with little experience whose only ammunition is a low commission. "In a few months," she says, "they disappear from the business and we never hear from them again. I know some people only buy at cut-rate prices. That's why there's a Wal-Mart. I tell my clients, 'If I let you sit here tonight and negotiate my commission away, how in the world could you ever trust me to be out there negotiating for every last penny of your equity?'"

Phyllis hears two other reasons for why prospective customers do not list their homes with her: that the seller has a friend in the business, and that a competing agent suggested to a prospect that Phyllis's phenomenal volume makes her too busy to serve them. "I tell people, 'If you want to stay good friends, keep them out of your serious real estate transactions.' As to the second charge I tell people, 'I *am* busy. Busy doing my job of selling more homes than anyone else in the state of North Carolina. That's the kind of person you need, one with a proven track record.'"

Even with that formidable success record, Phyllis finds she still has to work hard for every client. When she does lose a customer, she says, "You learn what you did wrong, shake it off, and simply start over again. I never count what I lost. I refocus on doing my best the next time." Phyllis is adamant that sales professionals should not dwell on negatives. "It ruins your day," she says. "I don't like war stories. Look, if you go to enlist in the Army, they don't tell you about Vietnam, do they? Why should I retain memories of my losses?"

Where Salespeople Fail

Throughout her career, Phyllis has come in contact with hundreds of other Realtors, both in her company and others, and she has been able to see their strengths and weaknesses. "Too many agents starting out today forget that real estate is a personable people business. Their goal is to sell a house. A billy goat could sell one house! Not one of these plaques came from selling a house. You have to look at this as a long haul, relationship-building business."

She sees many pleasant salespeople whose lack of confidence ruins any hope for success. She says that many newer agents will bury themselves in the technical details, such as the multiple listing service (MLS) computer, rather than doing marketing and talking to customers personally. Phyllis relates:

> I was selling $14 million a year before I knew how to turn the computer on and off. Forget the computer! I have never seen a computer buy a house. It will not bring you customers. That should be your primary focus. Get out there and visit homes on the market. Know the neighborhoods, the price ranges, the differences between models. That will give you confidence. Then spend every moment you can getting the word out that you are a serious, knowledgeable, committed player. You need customers to become successful. Then anyone can show you how to run the computer. I don't care how much technical knowledge you have. If you take away the human qualities, you are going to starve.
>
> I pride myself on being the expert on residential property in my area. I will drive customers through a neighborhood and tell them, "This house sold two years ago for $210,000," or "Brian Church built this home." People want to buy from me because I know my business. Hell, you can hire somebody to run the computer!

Sharing the Administrative Load

When her volume topped $15 million, Phyllis's managing broker convinced her to hire an assistant. Today, her assistant has an assistant. Phyllis is still the only person who works with buyers and sellers on listings, home selection, and closings, but her two assistants, Felice Ryals and

Donna Riordan, process the enormous amount of paperwork. They order signs, place ads, order home inspections, and monitor mortgage applications, Phyllis explains. "I would be absolutely lost without them. They are my two right hands. I just love them and think of them as my own family. We all think the same way."

Despite her initial reluctance, Phyllis believes her investment in hiring assistants to take care of the time-consuming administrative work was one of the biggest reasons her production leapt to new heights. Since her most important, and profitable, asset is her own time, freeing herself from the administrative details enabled her to devote more of her attention to dealing with prospects and clients.

Setting Goals

Despite her confidence in front of clients, Phyllis harbors some of the same fears shared by many other salespeople. "The sky is just so high," she reflects. "I create some of my own biggest barriers. I'm a 52-year-old woman and I'm so afraid that I'll set such a high goal for myself one year that I won't be able to make it." And what does she do when she does not reach the goals she set? "You can't beat yourself up," she answers. "I set my goals inch by inch, day by day. On January 1st I don't say 'I'm going to do X million this year.' I establish goals at the point where I've got something to strive for, but making my sales a primary objective changes the focus from satisfying the client to simply producing numbers. I don't want to make myself number one, I always want to concentrate on making my customer number one. Then all the rest will follow."

Barriers to Success

Like many salespeople, Phyllis occasionally has down times. When she encounters such periods, she sits with

Bernie and they talk it out. "I really don't call it a rut," she says. "There are emotional peaks and valleys, though. When I find myself in a down mood, I find it very helpful to try and remember the last one, and do you know that in just about every case, I can remember that the next day was so much better that I'm able to just put my present worries out of my mind. I try to focus on as much positive stuff as I possibly can. I'll go for a walk, read a book, eat something good, take a nap—then I find it goes away."

Sales superstars do not get all the opportunities they pursue, and they are plagued by the same doubts and fears that other, mere mortal, salespeople experience. The difference is that the superstar recognizes the problem and deals with it. Superstars simply do not let minor irritations become barriers along their road to success.

Making Customers Happy

Phyllis Wolborsky says that there is not a day in her life that she does not spend time thinking about how to get new business. By far the biggest source of new business is referrals from satisfied clients. After settlement, when the customer expresses their appreciation for her help throughout the sale process, Phyllis tells them that a personal referral is the highest compliment they can give her.

When asked about the most important things necessary to make a customer happy, Phyllis answers without a moment's hesitation. "Your knowledge of the product in the area they are interested in, your genuine concern for that person and their family, and your interest in more than just a sale." Her creativity, resourcefulness, and willingness to be more than a Realtor have cemented many long-term relationships with past customers. "I've been a cook, a baby-sitter, and a chauffeur," she says. "I've even been a banker, lending a seller the money to paint a house or re-carpet a room so it would show better when I listed the property."

With her stellar record, people frequently ask her why she doesn't open her own real estate agency. "Oh, *please!*" she exclaims. "I don't know how I'd do, having to manage people and worrying about whether they turned the lights off at night. Who knows what the future will bring, but in the meantime, it's like I said before, you have to concentrate on doing what you do best. I do one thing well: I help people buy and sell homes."

Coming from this housewife who let herself be talked into attending real estate school—and became the first agent in the country to be inducted into the Better Homes and Gardens Hall of Fame—that is an understatement if ever there was one. With no formal college or business training, she was named one of the Magnificent Seven in the real estate profession at the 1994 National Association of Realtors convention. She was also featured in the *Chicago Tribune* as one of the most prominent Realtors in the country. Phyllis Wolborsky simply loves what she does for a living. Her momentary mood of reflection vanishes as she takes a telephone call from someone at a local radio station. "There are lots of truly fine Realtors," she assures him, "but there's only one Phyllis." Indeed there is.

Irma Skaggs

★

Superstar from America's Heartland

When asked to conjure up images of sales superstars, you might think of Wall Street wonders and Realtors selling Beverly Hills estates. Yet far from the concrete jungles and the power lunches with millionaire clients, hours from even an interstate highway, lives Irma Skaggs, a superstar by any measure. Her home is in southeastern Iowa, where the road names change from numbers to letters and finally disappear altogether on the remote gravel byways. She began her sales career in a sparsely populated community, having no previous business experience. She was terrified of meeting new people, yet quickly became the top-selling salesperson in her district of 300.

Irma was born and raised in these rich, gently undulating farmlands. She received her education in a tiny one-room schoolhouse. There were only five to eight students in the entire school, and she was the only one in her grade. Perhaps it was this lack of interaction with other children her own age that caused the acute shyness she has carried for most of her 68 years. At the age of 18 she met her future husband, Howard Skaggs, at a roller skating rink. She became a farmer's wife and, eventually, a mother to three daughters and a son. Irma not only kept house and raised her children, but also cooked meals for the farm hands.

"Back in those days we had no electricity or running water, and I had to milk the cows by hand," she recalls, letting out a howl at the suggestion that it must have been hard work. "We didn't know any better back then, but I wouldn't change a thing if I had to do it all again." In the early sixties she began to yearn for a bit of freedom from the dawn-to-dark chores of the farm. Then in 1962, her sister-in-law recruited her to be an Avon lady.

The Beginning of a Career

"I never did it for the money," she says firmly. "I joined Avon so I could get out of the house at lunchtime." Her shyness was a problem, almost to the point of being an obsession. She remembers being uncomfortable around people as a young child. "Even in Sunday School or church, I used to get what today they call a 'panic attack.' At events where we were all called on to help, I always chose to do chores behind the scenes, where there were no other people. I just had a total lack of confidence in myself." It is hard to imagine how Irma thought she would succeed in sales with such a psychological handicap.

The day before she started with Avon, an incident occurred that affected the way she would deal with customers for the next 30 years. "This Fuller Brush salesman knocked on my door and wanted to come in and show his wares," recalls Irma. When she refused, he became ever more insistent. Finally, the no-nonsense farmer's wife became so angry that she slammed the door in the salesman's face and locked it—something she has never repeated.

"As I started my calls selling Avon, I was petrified people would say 'No,' or worse, that they would slam the door in *my* face," she admits. "But that never happened." Three decades later, she still remembers her first sales success: Avon's "Here's to My Heart" cream sachet, of which she sold 77 packets for 77 cents apiece. As new customers

became her friends, they referred their friends to her and her sales increased. She began to overcome her lifelong shyness and lack of confidence. Before long, Irma Skaggs was selling about $8,000 annually, an impressive figure in the sixties, especially considering that her rural community's population was only about 400.

A hallmark of Avon's service is that the representative personally delivers orders to the customers. Although Irma used her Avon deliveries to escape the noontime cooking chores, she never let it interfere with her obligations as a mother. "My kids never once got on the school bus when I was not there with them. I can also count on one hand the number of times when I was not there when they returned," she says. The four children were very active in extracurricular activities, and Irma would interrupt her Avon duties to drive them around. "I never missed a single game in any sport for any child," she states proudly. "That's why I liked Avon so much. I got to set my own hours."

Irma Skaggs operated her rural delivery routes as if they were published scheduled runs. If she had an obligation to drive the children somewhere, she would curtail the time she spent at each house, but she always called on every customer. Remembering her encounter with the pushy Fuller Brush salesman, Irma's attitude was always non-aggressive and never threatening. She always displayed the same polite, friendly Midwestern demeanor whether the customer bought anything or not. As time passed, not only did her sales grow, but every one of her customers became a friend.

In tiny Libertyville, Iowa, there were several elderly residents who bought very little from her but appreciated her visits. On long summer evenings, when Howard would be working in the fields until 10 P.M. or later, Irma would spend time visiting with them. "They just loved me for those long hours of fellowship and companionship," she smiles. "You see, I never thought of any customer in terms of sales. They're just nice folks I like to visit. If they buy from me, that's fine. If they don't, well that's OK too."

Ultimately, people would always buy from Irma. In 30 years of selling Avon products, the only person who repeatedly turned her down was a lady who received all of her personal care products from her daughter, a beautician. Yet Irma Skaggs never stopped dropping by to visit. "That's the difference out here in Iowa," she adds. "In the big city you don't even know your next-door neighbor. Here, people really appreciate the time you spend with them." Long before management gurus wrote books about "relationship selling," Irma Skaggs practiced it instinctively in America's heartland.

She has never had any formal training in selling skills, yet she claims to have never felt challenged by situations she encountered in her vocation. "The sale was never the most important thing to me," she says. "I can't explain why, but I never had any feelings of *having* to make that sale. I always just appreciated the time I spent with each customer. My customers—my friends—are what kept me going all the time I was sick."

Her Battle with Back Pain

For many years Irma had suffered from increasingly intense bouts of severe pain from a pinched nerve in her back, and she went for surgery in 1980. Unfortunately, when the surgeon scraped arthritic spurs from two of her vertebrae, he overdid it, breaking the vertebrae. The pain became excruciating. After returning home, she tried delivering to her Avon customers, but the pain was too great for her to even sit in her car. She was homebound.

By 1982, Irma was back in the hospital. The doctors attempted to fuse the broken vertebrae with some bone they had removed from her hip, but it was unsuccessful. Orthopedists at the University of Iowa Hospital and the famed Mayo Clinic told her that there was only one slim chance for avoiding a lifetime in a wheelchair: to undergo interbody fusion surgery—which they had never performed. "They sent me home and told me to wait until the pain was absolutely intolerable," she shudders. "I was in severe pain every waking minute of every day. By 1987, I realized I had to do something. My body and my mind were deteriorating. I was so irritable I could not stand being around people anymore. I couldn't stand or sit without pain, and I hated other people to see me that way." Her life was in constant disarray. She remembers she felt worst when her family would return home and she was unable to prepare a meal. Irma watched her sales drop far below the levels she had attained when she was able to visit customers and demonstrate new products.

In February 1988, Irma Skaggs presented herself to Dr. Keith Bridwell, an orthopedic surgeon at Barnes Hospital in St. Louis, Missouri, for her third operation. In seven hours of surgery, Dr. Bridwell's team fused her severed vertebrae with more bone scraped from her hip, holding it all together with two rods and six screws. She required another operation six weeks later, and more surgery two weeks after that. Irma was then put in a full body cast and was instructed to lie completely still in her hospital bed.

For most salespeople, this kind of pain, fear, and immobility would certainly take the wind out of their sails. Irma Skaggs is not just any salesperson, however. Although she was unable to move an inch inside her body cast, she talked to the doctors, nurses, and hospital staff about Avon's products. It did not take long for them to start placing orders with her. At the end of each day, Irma would call the orders in to the company, and the merchandise would be shipped to her home. When Howard made the next four-and-a-half-hour trip to St. Louis, he would bring the orders and she would distribute them to the Barnes Hospital workers.

When she finally returned home, she was still in the body cast. For many months she spent night and day in a rented hospital bed in her living room. This vibrant, strong woman hated for people to see her that way, and she says she will forever remember the eyes of her grandchildren when they saw her lying so immobilized. Still, it takes more than a full body cast to stop Irma Skaggs!

Her Office in Bed

She had the telephone and all of her files and catalogs brought to her bed, and she used a beanbag tray-table as a desk top. Every day, Irma would call her customers, verbally making the rounds of what used to be her delivery route. She paid a friend to sort the incoming shipments and drop off the orders, and she slowly rebuilt her business. "My bed was full," she laughs. "I had the telephone, the bean-bag board, all my books and records—even a ledge to hold the adding machine."

In December 1988, ten months after her first surgery, the doctors removed the body cast, and, through physical therapy, Irma slowly began to recover. She discovered, however, that the many months of pain, solitude, and embarrassment had caused her childhood shyness to reappear. "I was scared to death to go out and meet people again," she says. Yet her dogged determination helped her to overcome her timidity. "I am convinced that it was my love of selling Avon that helped me pull through," she adds.

Irma says she had always enjoyed the Avon sales meetings, and when she was able to drive, she began attending them again. Irma found that during the years of her poor health Avon had changed and expanded its entire product mix. Irma had to almost start from scratch. As her business began to grow again, two events catapulted Irma into the forefront of all Avon representatives in the country.

Moving to the Next Level

"When the company first came out with a jewelry line, I took it around to all my customers, but nobody bought a single thing," she recalls. "So when I got home, I said to myself, 'Irma, what are you going to do to stimulate some sales here?' I remembered that several people had liked the jewelry, but they had thought the prices were a little high. So the next day I went out and showed the jewelry again, this time telling them I would give them a discount on their purchase." She sold out her entire inventory. From that day on, Irma has given every customer a discount—

which comes out of her commission—on all of Avon's products.

Miki Crowl became Irma's Avon district manager in 1989. Just as Irma was beginning to recover, Miki approached her about an incentive trip to Maui, Hawaii. "I had been a trip winner several times when I was a representative," says the district manager, "and I found them to be very exciting. Avon always treated the trip winners so well, I couldn't understand why the trips did not motivate many more salespeople." She told Irma that she wanted to help her if Irma was willing to help herself.

Miki Crowl assured Irma that she could meet the high qualifications for the trip, and suddenly Irma found herself focusing on a destination beyond Iowa's amber waves of grain. "I give her all the credit," Irma says today. "She opened up an inner voice in me that kept saying, 'I will do this or I will die trying.' Don't ever tell me I cannot do something." Although she now had the motivation to sell the volume needed to qualify for the trip, Irma still never broke that down into goals per day or per customer. "Being number one was not, and is not, a motivator for me," she explains. "I never even added up my orders to see how I was doing. I just went out every day and did my best, and whatever happened, happened. I have always been a person who simply did my very best at whatever I was doing. If that makes me number five, it will not upset me." She looks bemused as she adds that she sees some people "ready to kill" to be number one. "That is not the most important thing in my life," she says. "The most important thing is enjoying life."

Recognition from the Top

Irma won the trip to Hawaii, and her life was changed because of it. She has long surpassed the $8,000 she sold annually in the days before her operations. Today she sells more than 20 times that much and has customers calling in orders regularly from as far away as California. Avon has rewarded Irma for her hard work, sending her on trips to Nashville, New Orleans, Orlando, Nassau, and Kona, Hawaii. Nevertheless, her Midwestern modesty steps in as she quickly adds, "But if it had not been for Miki Crowl, I would have been content producing my $8,000 a year in sales."

In 1994, Irma Skaggs was the recipient of Avon's Women of Enterprise Award. The company flew Irma and her family to New York, where she was honored in front of hundreds of other Avon salespeople. She had dinner with Barbara Walters and then stood in the spotlights and received the award from Jim Preston, the president of Avon. It was an impressive achievement for this Iowa farm wife who comes from a county that does not have a single stoplight.

Perilous Predicaments

On the road to success, most sales superstars encounter obstacles such as protective receptionists and annoyances such as telephone calls that are not returned. Irma's challenges were more physical. She has been chased by a billy goat that climbed right onto the roof of her car, has found a 500-pound calf stuck on the back porch of a customer's home, and has had to climb to the top of her car to escape from two attacking dogs. None of these incidents stopped her from making her appointed rounds, however. "I would go out to see customers on days when the weather was so bad there were no mail deliveries and school was canceled," she laughs, omitting the fact that sometimes Howard had to bring the tractor to pull her out of a snow drift.

"Irma was so used to hearing people tell her negative things, like 'You can't do that, slow down' and 'Don't try this, you might hurt your back,' that once she tasted sales success it gave her the confidence to really do well," says Miki Crowl. "Then there was no stopping her! Still, Irma also devotes much of her time to helping other Avon representatives. She is always willing to help new reps get started. She is *the* neatest lady."

The Qualities of a Salesperson

After three decades of a stellar sales career, what does Irma Skaggs believe are the primary attributes of a good salesperson? "It is simple," she says. "Being responsible, being dependable, and being honest." She seems surprised that one would even have to ask. What does she think is the biggest barrier that prevents other salespeople from attaining her levels of success? "They don't have the gumption," she declares. "They could do it if they wanted, my goodness they could easily sell more than me." For Irma, though, there is something worse than not performing. "Some people are not only content with mediocrity, they criticize those who *do* perform."

Miki Crowl notes that about 50 percent of her sales representatives drop out within a few months. Of the 300 or so in her five-county area, the average person produces only about $5,000 in annual sales. "So many people just have no confidence in themselves," she says. "Most of them are happy just doing their own thing. They do not want to take the risks involved in reaching for the bigger goals."

So what is *Irma's* barrier to even greater achievement? "I am almost 69," she says, in a moment of uncharacteristic melancholy. "My body is wearing out and this business has grown so big. I just don't know how I can build it much larger. I ship all over Iowa, Missouri, and Illinois as it is."

Lessons for Other Salespeople

What can the aspiring sales superstar learn from Irma Skaggs? Perhaps one of the essential lessons is that you can succeed regardless of your background, education, or location. What is important is that if you perform your job well, treat your customers right, be honest, and love what you do, the success will follow.

When Irma Skaggs looks back over her 69 years, she must surely feel content. Her children are all engaged in successful careers: Linda owns a television and appliance store, Marsha supervises a hospital x-ray unit, Randy is a schoolteacher, and Janet owns an interior design business. Her husband, Howard, is retired now, which in Birmingham, Iowa, means he only farms 135 acres, and her six surgeries have cured much of her back pain. Money was not what motivated Irma Skaggs to become an Avon representative in 1962, and it has never been particularly important in the decades since. For her, the rewards of 30 years of sales success are not tangible. She talks about the friendships she has formed and about how being an Avon sales representative has gotten her out of the kitchen and has helped her to shed her almost phobic shyness and low self-esteem.

The pride that comes from her selling skills and her relationship building shows when she talks about her very first trip to Hawaii as an Avon winner. "Howard and I went out onto the balcony of our hotel on Maui, and I felt as if Ed McMahon had just brought a million dollars to my house," she says. "As long as I live, I will never forget how I felt at that moment as we looked out across the Pacific at the most beautiful sunset I have ever seen. I felt as if I were in a dream . . . " Her voice, usually so strong, softens and then trails off as she relives that idyllic moment. "Too many good things have happened to me," she declares. "Nobody could ever comprehend the happiness this job has brought me." As her voice falters, the interviewer realizes that her eyes are glistening. It is a tender moment, and neither person knows quite what to say.

The telephone's shrill voice pierces the farmhouse kitchen. "Yes!" says Irma. "OK, fine. OK, OK. Well, thank you for the order. I will take care of it." And everybody— the interviewer, Avon, and especially the customer—knows she certainly will.

John Thackrah

DuPont's Veteran Superstar

Although every salesperson featured in this book is a superstar, each one approached the interviews with the author differently. Some brought published articles describing their accomplishments, others came to the meeting with a resume. Most simply said, "What do you need to know about me?" John Thackrah was unique. He arrived 25 minutes early. He was impeccably—if conservatively—dressed. He said, "I anticipated what you might want to ask me and I made this up for you," as he offered a bound 25-page custom-prepared binder filled with important career achievements. John Thackrah is a salesperson from the old school. He trained over 40 years ago and came up through the ranks of one of America's most venerable firms. His dress and manner of speech are polite and proper, and he believes in hard work and loyalty. Whether you meet him on an airplane or in the purchasing department, chances are you will immediately like and trust him. After all, his customers have for the last 41 years.

In 1953, when he was a senior in high school, John Thackrah was recruited by the DuPont Company as a sales trainee. "Back then, DuPont required a long training period before they let you go near a customer," he recalls. "The company put me in the plant so I would learn the product. Then they gradually introduced sales concepts and skills.

Along the way they built up my confidence and self-esteem so that when I hit the street they had convinced me I was one of the most important people in the DuPont Company. It was an 18-month training period back then; today training is done in six weeks." While conceding the importance of policies that improve the bottom line, Thackrah believes corporate America is missing something important by rushing entry-level salespeople onto the streets. He thinks that the earlier training methods with mentoring, coaching, and counseling helped the salespeople serve their customers more professionally.

Early Lessons

He remembers his first front-line sales assignment clearly. "It was in the New York office," he says. "My boss handed me a stack of 25 invoices and said, 'Go out and find these companies. Learn why they are buying from us and try to sell them more.'" It was hardly exciting work, but discovering why existing customers liked his product and service helped him in the years ahead when a prospect would ask, "Why should I buy from you?"

Just as he feels that first exercise was good training for his long career in sales, he believes it is sales itself that is the ideal preparation for management. "The people who are the worst bosses are those who have never sold," he declares. "They have never been thrown out of a sales call, have never been in a competitive situation with opposing personality types, and have never had to make a quick business decision. Rejection is a very powerful teacher, and salespeople deal with it every day. They have to know how to handle it. There is no committee to fall back on."

As he recalls his four decades of being a sales representative for DuPont, John Thackrah admits that not every experience was one from which he could later draw inspiration. One day Sid Kahn, DuPont's New York district manager, walked into the bullpen with another gentleman

and a dog. The only salesperson there was Thackrah, then the low man on the totem pole, and the district manager asked him for an unusual favor. He told Thackrah that the gentleman he was with was one of the company's best customers and the dog was the customer's prize boxer. The dog had a white spot on its nose, and the district manager said that every time the dog was entered in a show, the judges deducted 10 points for the spot. He told Thackrah that while he and the customer were at lunch, he wanted Thackrah to take care of the white spot.

As the two executives walked away, a stunned John Thackrah saw his future DuPont career hanging in the balance. "Now you have to understand," he says, "this was the Great White Father. The Big Boss. So when he said, 'Jump!' your only response was, 'Yes, sir! How high?'"

Deciding it was time for technical help, he trotted down to the laboratory with the boxer. "I remember the face of the lab guy, Jimmy Loper, when I marched in with the boxer and explained the assignment," he laughs. They began mixing industrial dyes, and after a few attempts, came up with the right color. Then Loper held the back of the dog, while Thackrah held the dog's nose and applied the dye. John recalls, "I held a beaker of boiling hot black dye in one hand and the dog's nose in the other and thought, 'Thank God I got a job selling with one of the world's truly professional organizations or I do not know what I would be doing right now.' Anyway, the dog didn't bite us, he took the dye just fine. So fine, in fact, that his tongue came out and he licked it off the white spot. I don't know what Jimmy put in the dye, but every time I dabbed some on the dog's cheek he would lick it off. We finally applied enough so that the spot disappeared and I got back to the office just as the owner returned. He was really pleased. I guess he never noticed the dog's black tongue!" Perhaps this story had a lesson after all: when the customer asks for something to be done, use all your resourcefulness and creativity to deliver, no matter how unusual the request.

Advice from a Mentor

Thirty-one years ago John Thackrah attended the retirement party of his mentor, Fred "Cookie" Crayton, and the words of the veteran salesman on that occasion would stay with Thackrah throughout his career. "I remember Cookie saying, 'Forty years ago somebody told me that selling is easy. You just have to treat your customers like friends.' I do not take friendship lightly. I still exchange Christmas cards with people I called on 20 years ago." It was Cookie

Crayton who sat with the young John Thackrah one day, passing on advice that John never forgot. He told John that the three musts for successful selling are think, make friends, and work like hell, but that they absolutely must be done in that order. "He told me that this rule had been passed on to him when he started with DuPont 44 years earlier," Thackrah recalls. "I have been using it since Cookie passed it on to me 31 years ago, so it is now a 75-year-old story. I hope one of the young salespeople I have told it to carries it on, because do you know what? It really works. Every time I analyze a sale that I won, I find I've followed the rule, in the right order. When I try to figure out why I lost an order, I discover that I blew Cookie's advice."

Now John Thackrah is retiring from DuPont after about the same tenure as his mentor, and insists that Cookie's rule still applies today. He still believes that salespeople should not worry about selling when they go into a prospective account; they should first concentrate on forming a relationship. If they build a clientele that likes and trusts them, the sales will follow. "The customer considers you a valuable resource to him," John explains. "You see, everyone has choices. When you buy something, don't you go to the stores you like doing business with? Your customer has choices of vendors for your product, too. So you need to establish the relationship where he likes you, trusts you, and chooses to give business to you."

A Love of Selling

John Thackrah truly loves selling. "I really believe I have the best job in the company, but then every successful salesperson will say the same thing." He offers a quotation from Adrienne Kardon, currently a rising sales star at DuPont: "Monday and Tuesday can be rotten days, but on Wednesday I can get up and experience the thrill of the hunt again." Thackrah says he has seen many good people in other industries get to a point in their careers when they are bored, but suggests that that is something that never happens with sales pros because they continue to find new challenges and continue to win new customers. He believes that by strengthening their relationships with existing clients every day, they are able to sell more.

John Thackrah's "Rules of Three" come from his 41 years of selling experience, with credit to Cookie Crayton for the first one:

Three Musts for Successful Selling
1. Think
2. Make friends with your customers
3. Work like hell

Three Lessons from Sales
1. You learn humility
2. You learn that sales is the best job in the world
3. You learn that customers are great and can be fun

Three Keys to Corporate Success
1. Doing your best every day
2. Helping those above you, beside you, and below you. If they get promoted due to your assistance, they may be in a position to help you in the future.
3. Luck

Three Critical Measures
1. Consistently deliver results
2. Maintain good relationships with people
3. Have a daily can-do attitude

Getting to the Customer

Although he has set forth these rules, John is quick to admit that he does not have all the secrets to sales success. Advice on building relationships will not help you if you cannot get in front of the buyer, a situation encountered frequently by many salespeople. Thackrah overcame this obstacle through creativity and dogged persistence. In one case, he had been trying to meet the purchasing manager of a potential customer in Statesville, Georgia, for an entire year. Every time John cold-called, the man told the receptionist he could not see him. When John made appointments and arrived at his office, the secretary would bring word that the manager had an urgent interruption and had canceled their meeting. Clearly, persistence was not working. It was time to use creativity.

John Thackrah found out where the purchasing manager lived and parked in front of his house one morning before dawn. At 6:00 A.M. the hall lights came on, the front door opened, and Mr. Big tip-toed down the front walk in his pajamas to pick up the newspaper. The big moment had arrived! Thackrah nimbly jumped from his car and walked up to the startled purchasing manager. "Who the hell are you?" asked the man. "I'm your friendly DuPont salesman, and for a year I have tried to meet you to give you a pen and some literature," Thackrah replied. The man looked dazed and then realized he was standing in the cold night air in his pajamas. "Good gosh," he sighed. "Anyone who wants to meet me this badly deserves a shot. Come on in for some coffee and breakfast." John Thackrah continues the story, "So we both went inside the house, and there was his wife in the kitchen in hair curlers and a bathrobe. She asked, 'Who is this?' and her husband said, 'Don't even ask. Just get us some coffee, please.'" The prospect became a DuPont customer. John Thackrah's creativity—and Cookie Crayton's sales formula—had worked to everybody's benefit.

On another occasion, John was again faced with a situation that required creativity and determination. He had been put off several times by the plant manager of a prospective customer in Atlanta. One day he was again sitting in the reception lounge hoping to receive an audience, but suspecting the worst. Then in walked three men. They told the receptionist that they were from the DuPont Company and that they had an appointment with the plant manager. John could hardly believe his ears. When the woman left to find the manager, John jumped to his feet. "You people are with DuPont?" he asked. "So am I. I'm with Dyes and Chemicals. Which division are you from?" He soon learned that this company had been an account of the DuPont Textile Fibers sales representative for years, and he told them of his inability to get in front of the very man with whom they had a relationship. He asked the other salesmen if they would do him a great favor and allow him to go in with them. He said he would not say a word while they conducted their business, but asked that they introduce him to the plant manager when they were done. To his delight, the salesmen agreed. When the receptionist returned, she ushered the foursome into the plant manager's office. "I just could not believe my luck," Thackrah chuckles. "I remember thinking, 'Boy, oh boy. This is my lucky day!'"

Once inside the manager's office, he noticed that the manager did not respond to the sales representatives' opening pleasantries and thought that perhaps he was hard of hearing. After a lengthy and increasingly uncomfortable silence, the buyer addressed the group. "I want to tell you people something," he said, pointing at the lead salesperson. "I have had it up to here with your crap and your lousy service. I don't like you. I don't like your company. I don't like your product, and I'm happy to tell you I have found a new supplier. Now get the hell out of my office, don't ever come back, and take your friend with you."

The four salesmen walked to the parking lot in total silence. Then Thackrah recalls telling them, "Well, thanks for your help, guys, but if it's OK with you, I'm perfectly capable of getting thrown out of my own accounts in the future." The anecdote would end there with most salespeople, but not with John Thackrah. He pondered the situation and then contacted the plant manager a week later, explaining who he was. His mettle so surprised the man that he granted Thackrah an appointment, which he kept. "I sold him!" declares a proud John Thackrah. "He was a customer for years after that."

Honesty with Yourself Is Critical

"You see, when you commit yourself daily to the profession of selling," he adds, "you will experience the thrill of the hunt and the joy of winning. Nevertheless, you will also have to endure the agony of defeat." Although no salesperson enjoys defeat, John Thackrah believes there is much to be learned from it. He teaches his salespeople to take the time to examine what they did right, and wrong, after they call on a customer or prospect. "I call it curbside reflection," he notes, "and even today, I teach our salespeople to do it after they finish every sales call." He cautions that this advice should not be taken lightly and that a casual recall of the visit while listening to the car radio should not be counted as curbside reflection.

"It is vital that you are brutally honest with yourself," he adds. "The toughest call I ever made to my boss in Atlanta was when I told him to take a customer away from me. They were a good account, but no matter what I did, I found that I was incompatible with the buyer. If I had said nothing, DuPont would have eventually lost the customer, and that would not have been fair to either company."

Expanded Territory

As Thackrah's sales grew, he progressed up the corporate ladder, but he always maintained relationships with DuPont salespeople and with his customers. Along with his increased responsibilities came a territory that extended far beyond his familiar beat. He had begun as a street-level salesperson, but through hard work and perseverance he sold himself into a career with a global territory.

In 1969, DuPont sent John Thackrah to Japan to promote a new line of textile printing dyes. Many other sales representatives, both with his firm and with their U.S. competitors, had tried and failed to make inroads into that market. With the help of Tony Yonei, the company's local representative in Japan, he succeeded in building a customer base.

Tony Yonei acted as translator for Thackrah while he was in Japan. Thackrah noticed that what Tony said to the Japanese customers was not a literal translation of the English he had spoken. Sometimes Thackrah would say two sentences, and the translator would utter a word or two. At other times, after speaking for just a few seconds in English, Thackrah watched his colleague speak in Japanese for several minutes. When they were alone, he asked Tony for an explanation. "It is not enough to simply translate the words," said Yonei. "I am turning what you say into language that is culturally acceptable to the Japanese."

After all his years in sales, John Thackrah was still learning how to make the perfect presentation! It was his persistence, his sensitivity to the customer's needs, and his understanding the need to be customer driven that enabled Thackrah to succeed where so many had failed. The lessons he learned in Japan helped make him a better salesperson in America. "Tony and I went on to be dear friends," he says. "He taught me much about cultural differences that I use to this day. We were from two different worlds, yet those worlds came together and benefited the customers, the company, and the two of us." Tony Yonei's patience and John Thackrah's perseverance led to millions of dollars in sales in that previously untapped marketplace.

Sales That Benefit All Concerned

In 1990, John Thackrah's persistence helped him make a sale that people in his industry still point to as a benchmark. It was a multimillion-dollar package that resulted in a joint venture between DuPont and CIBA Corporation to use Teflon for textiles. Although it was not the type of sale he was usually involved in, he saw an opportunity and took advantage of it. The deal took 18 months to negotiate, and there were times when people on both sides thought it was dead. "At low moments like that," Thackrah says, "I would always focus on my favorite quotation. In 1937, Winston Churchill gave the commencement address at Oxford University. Instead of the customary 30-minute speech, he stood at the podium in total silence. After several minutes, the tension from the audience was electric. Then Churchill, slowly, and in a voice that boomed louder with each syllable, said, 'Never, Never, NEVER, *N E V E R* give up!' That is all he said, but to me those words have inspired me so much because there is nothing else that needs adding. Those words gave me the motivation to continue." John Thackrah led the team that brought legal, technical, and financial gurus from both companies together time and again. The deal was finally signed, and the partnership has run smoothly and profitably ever since. "You see," he adds, with a note of triumph, "think, make friends, and work like hell! I did all of those things on this occasion, just as I did on the little deals. Everybody benefited; we all won. This was a contract worth tens of millions of dollars. The size of the deals may change, but the way you reach the sale, and the fun of selling, never do."

Although the basics of the deal must be driven by sound business principles, often the sale would never have been made without good interpersonal relationships. Thackrah points to the CIBA sale and another multi-million-dollar transaction with Britain's Associated Octel as examples of relationship selling. In the CIBA sale, Thackrah developed bonds with CIBA's Ed Kleiner in New York, Mario Christen in Switzerland, and Pharsee's Hanspeter Rafael in Germany. In the Associated Octel sale, the relationship he built was with the company's president, John Little, in London. "We'd battle like crazy to negotiate the best deal for our respective companies," he says, "but the relationships we had developed got us through the rough times. You see, if you don't understand and respond to the other side's needs, you'll never do the deal." He categorizes those business adversaries as people with whom he has maintained relationships of respect and mutual trust, and with whom he has very deep friendships. "I've been John Little's guest at Wimbleton, and he's been mine at the Masters," John adds. "It's a wonderful thing to develop such strong relationships with your customers that they become life-long friends."

Looking Back on 42 Years of Selling

It is only natural that at the end of 1994, as Thackrah prepared to retire from the only company for which he ever worked, he reflected back upon his career. He remembered the advice given to him by his manager when they transferred him to Atlanta in the fifties.

> The manager told me, "John, one of these days, you will be ready to go home at the end of a long, hard week, and the phone will ring. The guy on the other end will be a potential customer on the other side of the state saying he is interested in buying from DuPont, but he needs to see your dye samples—tonight. Then you will have a decision to make. Do you go home and say, 'I will take them Monday' or do you drive across the state right then and build up a few chips with that customer for the future? The choice is always yours, John. Just remember, if you decide to do extraordinary things for your customer, he or she will do similarly for you."

Managing in Changing Times

When asked to nominate candidates from DuPont for this book, Research and Development director Maury Snavely asked his organization whom they considered to be the best salesperson they had ever met. "The replies came back with a unanimous vote for John Thackrah," Snavely reports. "John can sell anybody anything. That is the best compliment the R&D organization can give to a man they all admire, respect, and trust."

John Thackrah remains a favorite mentor in the DuPont sales organization. He is considered paternal, yet streetwise; fair, but firm; creative and solution-minded, yet solidly reliable; a good company man, but also a great people person. His anecdotes are entertaining and instructional, but in the autumn of his career, Thackrah does not spend his days waxing poetic over his memories of the good old days. He is very much a modern manager, and he has equipped his team with the tools and the vision to take them into the next century. In 1986, he equipped every member of his sales force with portable computers. They now carry state-of-the-art laptops that provide instant global communication. "I remember how different it was just a few years ago," he says. "We would discuss products or competitive information at the annual sales meeting and then would go out on the road with the notes we had taken. Today in my strategic business unit [SBU], I have 65 different product lines that our 236 sales and marketing people sell worldwide. If I have a product update, a pricing change, or a nugget of competitive information, it goes out on E-mail to all 236 sales and marketing people around the world, and they can read it on their laptops within seconds. That is part of our competitive advantage."

Thackrah admits that it is very difficult for any one person to truly think globally. He says you have to focus on where you believe you can make things happen. Some products are gaining market share, others experience sudden pricing pressure. Good sales managers need to be very adept at communicating this information to their entire global team quickly. "Our only hope for success today and tomorrow is to be highly proficient in our use of the information superhighway," he adds. "We must perfect communications between our customers, the field sales people, and the company—in both directions."

Challenges for Sales Managers

Many salespeople will go on to become sales managers, just as Thackrah did. He cautions them to disregard the old model where a sales manager's primary task was to motivate the sales force to increase their production. Those who move into sales management still need to sell, but it is a different type of selling. John estimates that he spends 50 percent of his time selling, only now he does it by reading his salespeople's customer reports and then delivering his selling strategy to the customer through the salesperson.

He cautions that the sales process is far more complex than it used to be. It is critical that salespeople understand their markets, the values of their customers, and the classification of their products. For example, he says salespeople must ask themselves what is the size, the mix, and the profitability of the markets they serve? What are the strategies of each product line they market? Which are growth markets and where do they need to devote energy to maintain current levels?

He explains that his SBU has 29 identifiable markets, each classified according to type, potential, and profitability. "Once you communicate your salable core competencies and your salespeople understand them, you can whip the competition by having everybody on your team pull together." He says that a sales manager in the nineties needs to understand the market and his product classifications, must communicate the company's core competency, and then link them together to take advantage of the identifiable growth opportunities.

It would be trite to say "they don't make them like him anymore." It would also be sad. For John Thackrah is the type of salesperson whose integrity, grit, and sheer will to win has helped turn many American businesses into global industry leaders. This man has perhaps heard "No" more times than anyone in business. Because he went right on thinking, making friends, and working like hell, however, he also had more customers say "Yes" than any of his peers. This is a sales superstar. John Thackrah started selling by "hollering up elevator shafts in Brooklyn." He ended his career as sales and marketing director of DuPont's $2 billion Specialty Chemicals Division's strategic business unit, managing a global sales force of 100. Ned Jackson, DuPont vice president, calls John Thackrah "the consummate salesperson. He eats, drinks, and sleeps selling." He says that John may not be Tom Peters, Lee Iacocca, or some other famous selling character, "but in my book he is one of the most persistent, innovative, and exciting sellers I have worked with in my 33 years in the chemical industry."

On the day he retired, December 31, 1994, nothing would have given Thackrah a bigger thrill than for his most junior sales trainee to have come to him, saying, "Hey, John, would you come with me on a sales call this afternoon? I really think we can get this prospect as a new customer." Then the retirement party would have had to wait a while. After John made the sale, inspiring the young trainee who represents the next generation of sales professionals, the superstar would go to the party—probably with his new customer, who by then had become a friend.

Sid Friedman

★

The Rolls Royce of Life Insurance Salesmen

"It's the white Rolls Royce," Sid Friedman tells the valet at one of Atlantic City's opulent oceanfront hotels. "The convertible." Not bad for the kid from a working-class neighborhood in Boro Park, Brooklyn. The lifestyle he enjoys today—the Rolls (usually driven by a chauffeur); the expensive jewelry; the mansion in fashionable Haddonfield, New Jersey; and the first-class flights to exotic destinations—comes from his incredible ability to sell life insurance policies.

In any year in this or any other recent decade, Sidney A. Friedman has been the top-selling agent and the manager of the top-selling agency in at least one of the nation's premier life insurance companies. He has become an industry leader who now devotes a substantial part of his time to helping others attain their own goals. Friedman's success is the result of a quarter century of incredible energy that is responsible for his drive, his strong work ethic, and his personal goal setting. He is also one of a rare breed of self-made superstars who have been able to motivate others to their peak potential.

Friedman's strong work ethic and the help he received from others early in his career have been keys to his success. Perhaps these are the reasons that he is so willing to share his techniques with both aspiring salespeople in his

109

company and audiences of thousands around the country. As a teenager, Friedman went to work for his uncle, David Jacobs, who owned an insurance agency in Brooklyn. It was a deliberate move on his part, he recalls. "I looked around at everyone else in my family. He was the only one making money consistently."

After graduating from college, Friedman continued to work for his uncle while he earned a law degree at night school, and he had weekend gigs as a trumpet-playing band leader. He was successful in all three endeavors. "I earned $100,000 a year 35 years ago, and that was quite an achievement for someone my age," he notes. He was so successful at selling life insurance in his uncle's agency that he decided he deserved more recognition. "My uncle had his name in huge letters on my business cards, then in tiny type in the bottom corner it said 'Sidney A. Friedman.' So I asked him to give me cards with my name more prominently displayed." To Friedman's surprise, his uncle refused and the topic was closed to future discussion. That was when Friedman decided it was time to spread his wings.

A Job with a Promise

Sidney Friedman landed a job as a junior sales manager with the Phoenix Mutual Life Insurance Company, which became Phoenix Home Life after a merger in 1993. Before he was hired, Sidney had told his interviewers that he was not interested in being a salesman or low-level sales manager forever. His goal was to be an agency manager at one of the company's branches. After he was hired by Phoenix Home Life, he was told by the company that if he could reach a certain sales level within two years, a production target they did not expect him to attain, they would give him his own agency to manage. The Phoenix man-

ager did not know it at the time, but when Sid Friedman sets his sights on a goal, it is as good as met:

I found out later that they believed the objectives were almost impossible to reach. At the time, my wife, Sue, was six months pregnant with our first child, and that put me right into supercharge mode. I rose just after 5 A.M. and would be at my desk before 7:00 A.M. I never took a day off, and usually got home around 10 P.M. I worked with my agents. I went on calls with them, held sales meetings, helped with case development—whatever it took—six days a week. I was there to help them become successful because I earned an override on every dollar they brought in. Then on the seventh day, I did not rest. I spent it calling on personal clients whom I could not meet with during the week.

Six months later, a year and a half ahead of his target, Friedman notified Phoenix Mutual's management that he had met their goals. It was time for his own agency.

This Was a Reward?

The company probably thought they had the last laugh when they delivered on their side of the agreement. They assigned Friedman to the Philadelphia office, the lowest producing, most problem-plagued agency in the country. "When I first walked in here, I was shocked," he recalls today. "There was no management, no discipline, no morale—heck, there was no business! The 23 agents had, collectively, generated only $28,000 in commissions for the entire previous year. Most of them were characters I would not want to share an elevator with, let alone trust them to sell me life insurance."

Friedman's success in turning around the Philadelphia office was due to what he calls the "Sid Friedman Success System": Have a dream, plan your work, maintain discipline, and have the courage to do whatever it takes. He realized he had to start from scratch. After a month of working with the salespeople in the Philadelphia office, he had the information he needed and fired all but two of the agents. Some people would think Phoenix Mutual had given them a raw deal by putting them in charge of Philadelphia's Keystone Agency back then. Sid believed he could do nothing but succeed because the office could sink no further.

Once again he took on the challenges of building his personal sales and recruiting a team of professional salespeople. The news that he had terminated almost the entire agency sales force spread throughout the industry like wildfire. He knew he had taken a radical step, yet he realized that the future success of the entire agency, and therefore of his own career, was solely his responsibility.

Early in his career Friedman coined the phrase "If it is to be, it is up to me" and says those 10 simple two-letter words have guided him ever since. Today he imparts this tip for success to those who come to hear him speak at industry conventions. "You have to take responsibility for yourself, your career," he says. "A sales manager can help you, can be a resource, but ultimately you are the one who decides what time to set the alarm or what time to quit every day. It was like that when I first came to the Philadelphia office. If I failed and became the laughing stock of the company, who would I blame? I knew I could turn this place around. I accepted the challenge and took responsibility for doing it. If it is to be, it is up to me. The rule applies today, just as it did 30 years ago."

Setting Lofty Goals

One of the keys to Friedman's success was his ability to set goals for himself and then to work doggedly to achieve them. Sales trainers have stressed the importance of goal setting for those who sell for a living. Goals can be a numerical standard, such as a dollar amount of sales or an income to be reached. They can also be a reward reaped upon achieving a certain level of success, such as a vacation to Cancun. Trainers stress that whatever goal is chosen must be quantifiable and expressed in writing, and the reward must be of high value to the person setting the goal.

One of Sid's goals was to own a Rolls Royce. It had been a dream of his since he was a child, and long before he ever rode in one, or even knew their cost, he pledged that he would own one before his 40th birthday. As he went about building his personal sales and recruiting new agents for the Philadelphia office, he reaffirmed his childhood aspiration of owning the car of kings before he was 40. He had 18 months to do it.

"I was still working six days a week—sometimes seven," he recalls. "I'd be in the office by 7:00 A.M. and would hold the agency sales meetings at 7:30. By 8:30 we were all primed, motivated, and usually at our first appointments. I never forgot my dream of the Rolls Royce, but to make a dream into a reachable goal, you have to make it appear real." One Saturday each month, Sidney would spend the day with his four-year-old daughter, Lori. They would dress in their best clothes and drive to Manhattan for lunch. Then they would visit the Rolls Royce dealership and "their" car. The car salesman would recognize him and would stay clear of this strange fellow from Philadelphia. For two or three hours, Sid and Lori would sit in the luxurious vehicle parked in the showroom. He would run his hands across the smooth, solid mahogany dashboard and would close the door a few times to hear the solid "clunk." He would shut his eyes and inhale as he stored the memory of the rich aroma of the leather seats and would surround himself with the resonant sound of the car's stereo system. Then they would drive home.

Those visits were part of what he needed to help keep his dream vivid and real. When he was tempted to stay in bed in the mornings, the memory of that Mozart violin concerto playing in the Rolls Royce would motivate him to get to work. When he would head for home a little early because of a heavy snowfall in the afternoon, he would remember the distinctive smell of the supple leather interior and would be inspired to pull over and make another hour or so of sales calls. Fourteen months after his first visit to the dealership, just 120 days before his 40th birthday, Sid Friedman proudly strode into the showroom and paid cash for his Rolls Royce, the first of many. He had made his dream come alive.

Friedman's personal sales continued to increase, and he began to receive recognition for his accomplishments. He first qualified for the Million Dollar Round Table, an award earned by agents who sell life insurance in amounts far above the industry average. He went on to qualify for the Court of the Table, and then earned the highest award in the industry, the Top of the Table. Based strictly on the sales volume of policies sold that year, the Top of the Table is bestowed upon only one-tenth of one percent of life insurance agents each year. "Of the 500,000 agents who sell life insurance worldwide, fewer than 500 made Top of the Table last year," he says. "Most cities don't have a single person who made the cut. We had four from this office." Sid is one of only 24 agents in the world whose sales have qualified him for the Top of the Table in each of the 19 years the award has been in existence.

Attracting Quality Salespeople

Attracting agents with either great potential or a substantial amount of existing business is one of an agency manager's primary duties. Other industry managers, finding themselves, as Sid Friedman did, with practically no sales agents, would recruit almost anyone who walked in. One sales manager at another agency exemplified this attitude when he said, "Let's assume you hire an agent and they sell a policy to themselves, their father, and their sister. Then they leave the business in six months because they can't hack it. If we go through 10 agents a year like that, that's 30 policies a year we've put on the books." This is not how Friedman thought. Just as Sid Friedman had set his sights on a car that was the top of the line, so he began attracting only the cream of the crop when he recruited sales agents.

His fortitude paid off. Today the Keystone Agency is perennially the top-selling office out of the 60 in Phoenix Home Life's nationwide network. In 1994, his 50 agents generated over $6 million in premiums for sales of their sponsor's policies, plus many millions more in sales of other carriers' policies. In a business where a few hundred dollars in annual sales often separates one agency from the next, Keystone was 40 percent higher than the second-ranked office.

Sid will not pay a new agent the customary training allowance stipend. "If you bought a McDonalds or 7-11 franchise, they wouldn't send you a check for two years while you got your business established. In fact, you'd have to send them a check," he reasons. "This business is similar. You are starting your own practice here. I won't make you give me a check every month, but why should I pay you when I'm already giving you free office space, secretarial help, management expertise, and so on?" Before a salesperson new to the industry is hired, on pure commission, they must prove to Sid that they have at least 12 months' living expenses available in cash.

The industry average for a life insurance agent's earnings is around $30,000. Friedman will not consider hiring an agent unless he feels they can qualify for the President's Club by earning about $50,000 in commissions after their first year in the business, and he will not keep an agent who cannot achieve this level of sales. "I want them to be making a minimum of $150,000 after three years and $250,000 a year after five years," he adds. "And that's not the good ones. I'm talking about average agents."

His oldest daughter, Lori, joined him at the Keystone Agency as a salesperson six years ago and is already proving the adage that the acorn does not fall far from the tree. "She has already qualified for the Million Dollar Round Table three times," the proud father reveals. He notes that when she began, she was going after the same type of business every life insurance agent does. She would ask everyone she met—waitresses, cab drivers, etc.—if they wanted to buy life insurance. "Then she got smart, all by herself," he continues. "After six months she told me, 'This is nonsense! I only have so much time to give, so I should be devoting every hour to its most profitable use. I'm so busy trying to pick up pennies that I don't have the time to look for dollars.'" Friedman's daughter has now started to develop a very nice clientele of wealthy, high net-worth individuals.

Now He Can Put His Name in Large Type!

Today Sidney Friedman is the ultimate success story. He is the top manager every year, and his agency has had the highest sales and commission volume in the company every year for 15 straight years. A top producer in his own right, he enjoys a lifestyle befitting someone whose income is $1–$2 million a year. Yet he keeps on selling and continues to motivate others to achieve their own goals. "I have only two speeds," he says, "frantic and stop. Nothing gets in my way while I am working. When it is time to work, that is the only thing to be doing."

What does Sid see as barriers to success for most salespeople? "I see so many people using work time to socialize," he says. "I'm not talking about time to build client relationships, I'm talking about how too many salespeople stop to play in the middle of their day. That's a barrier that prevents them from ever getting into the big league, I believe. The real world of selling is cold-calling people and having them slam the phone down on you. So what? You can't take that? You can't take a hang-up from somebody you have never met and never will? Then get out of sales, because you shouldn't consider that to be a barrier to success." In baseball, he says, the difference between a Hall of Famer and the guy who gets fired is one more hit every so many times at bat. To get more hits, you have to take more swings. The same applies to the field of selling. To make more sales, you have to take more misses than the mediocre salesperson.

Tips on Sales Management

"I tell all my agents, 'You need to stop now and then and try to find the raisins in your rice pudding,'" he says. That phrase may sound cute, but salespeople who share an office with Friedman know that it is just another message from their mentor reminding them to be disciplined and results oriented.

Sid Friedman is no armchair executive who sits at his desk shuffling papers. He says that his agents know they can go to him with problems or for help with any case. They know that once they have asked him, he is going to give them straight answers. "If they screwed up, they are not going to like my answer because, as any one of them will tell you, I shoot with real bullets," he admits. "They know I will always be fair and honest with them . . ." A knock on the door of his luxurious corner office suite interrupts him. "I'm sorry to trouble you," says his secretary, "but Leon wanted me to let you know he sold that case and just brought in the application and check." One of his agents has just closed a life insurance sale whose $5,900 monthly premium will add another $35,000 to the agent's commission checks this year.

Friedman apologizes for the interruption, but it is obvious that the agent is king around his office, especially when they are bringing in such a pleasing sale. He chuckles and then recalls how there was a time when it would have been a really big deal for someone to bring in a $70,000 premium case. "Now," he says, "60 percent of the policies my agents sell are big cases."

Sid notes that the agents in his office have learned how to turn their excuses into opportunities. He says that now the salespeople in his agency even think like he does. With obvious pride he tells of days when there was two feet of snow on the ground and the city of Philadelphia had ground to a halt. Schools were closed, the mail stopped, and businesses told their employees not to come in. Yet when he made it into the office, the place was humming. All the successful agents had shown up because they sensed all those prospects who were stuck at home near the telephone. Those are the agents who look at a good blizzard as a gift. In fact, the more it snows, the prouder they are that they came in. Friedman says his philosophy is to find out what the whole world is doing, and then do the opposite.

"However, once you do agree to do something, you must make sure you deliver," he warns. "I have told the producers here for 30 years that the secret to satisfied clients is simple: promise a lot—then deliver more. Do that with your customers, do it with your family, do it for those above you and below you. Promise a lot, then deliver more."

Sid's Secrets of Success

Today this extremely confident, polished superstar has earned the right to express his opinion on the profession of selling. He believes that the major hurdle salespeople encounter is not wanting to pay the price for success. "They can dream all they want," he says. "They can sit in the office for days putting their plan together. Then they wait until tomorrow to press the start button. Nothing's ever going to happen until you press the start button."

Sid Friedman's experience in the sales industry is revealed in his many catchy aphorisms and success tips on the topics that interest the aspiring sales star:

Losing a sale. "It happens to me all the time, so I know it happens to you. When it does, just keep on going. Continue doing the things you know are right. We all go through peaks and valleys. The time when you really learn and become a better salesperson is after you have been beaten up. The peaks are full of the boring stuff."

Following the corporate culture. "If I did everything Home Office wanted, I would be number fifteen instead of number one."

The biggest sale he ever made. "I have not made it yet! Actually, that's Ben Feldman's line, but I love the message it carries."

Who motivates him. "Harvey McCay, (author of *How to Swim with the Sharks without Being Eaten*), Joe Weldon, Tony Robbins—he seems to really believe what he talks about."

Discipline. "Any salesperson worth their salt has to be disciplined in doing the routine, in this case, cold-calling. I insist that every agent in this office make 100 cold calls a week, every week. It's like going to the gym. If you go there and work out every day, you're going to get skinny. It's the price you are prepared to pay."

Marketing. "It is not good enough to have a great mousetrap. You have to tell people about it."

Being number one. "If you are not the lead dog, the view never changes."

Time management. "Your time is one factor that directly determines your income. If you set your alarm clock 50 minutes earlier, cut 20 minutes from your lunch break, and work 50 minutes later each day, that will give you 520 extra work hours a year. That is 13 additional 40-hour weeks you have just squeezed into your year! Even if you are only earning $75,000 a year, you have just added $18,000 to your income."

Closing. "Closing is not a separate process, it is the entire process. You begin closing the moment you say 'Hello.'"

Managing salespeople. "I am not especially smart. I treat people the way I like to be treated. That is not a cliché, I mean it. I tell the truth, I demand total ethical integrity from my people, and I try to catch them doing something right every day."

Favorite quotations. "If you aren't fired with enthusiasm, you will be fired with enthusiasm" (Vince Lombardi). "The three most important things: be good and know it, keep on getting better, and critique your own performance" (Larry Wilson). "You may be disappointed if you fail, but you are doomed if you don't even try" (Beverly Sills).

What Keeps His Motivation High?

To maintain his competitive edge, Friedman participates in an exclusive executive focus group four times a year. He networks with other high achievers and together they discuss the things that challenge and motivate them, and explore how they can take their personal development to the next level. "I have made more money and enjoyed more success than I ever dreamed was possible," he admits. "What motivates me now is doing a good job, being the absolute best I can be." Sid Friedman has illustrated that having a drive to succeed, working long hours, and pursuing one's goals pay off with handsome rewards. His success now attracts the best life insurance salespeople in the region. Anyone who is anyone wants to be associated with the Keystone Agency because success truly breeds success.

"Let me tell you something else that really charges me up," he adds. His voice drops, almost to a whisper, as if he has discovered something wondrous. He describes how he wanted to give something back, so he got involved in a charity called the Make a Wish Foundation. It tries to grant the wishes of children who are terminally ill, such as meeting the sports stars on a day at the ballpark or taking a trip to Disney World. Friedman now gives all the proceeds from his book and tape sales to them.

"A little while ago I heard about a six-year-old girl who had been crippled by multiple sclerosis, which was especially sad since her dream had always been to become a ballerina." He tells how the terminally ill child so moved him that he went to the world famous Pennsylvania Ballet Company, whose home is at the Academy of Music, next to his office. The superstar salesman went after one of the most important sales in his life, one from which he knew he would not earn a penny, yet would feel richly rewarded. "The entire ballet company volunteered to come in two hours before a performance," he says. "Then the little girl's mother wheeled her into the theater and onto the stage, where she met the prima ballerina. They took her to a dressing room and helped her change into a tutu and ballet slippers. Then for one hour the troupe danced, the orchestra played, and this beautiful little girl danced in her wheelchair. At the end, the prima ballerina presented *her* bouquet of red roses to one radiant, beaming child." His voice breaking, Sid turns away and stares out the window before he finishes. "Two months later she died. Her mother described those eight weeks as the happiest of her daughter's life because she had seen her dream come true."

Sid Friedman's sales success has put him in an enviable position today. After 30 years of setting goals and working hard to realize them, he can now enjoy the even greater reward of helping the dreams of others come true.

John Leahy

★

Flying High with Airbus

Any salesperson worth their salt is busy, often meeting with customers in a territory as large as two or three states. John Leahy's territory is the world. "I have to be in Bangkok on Monday and Beijing on Wednesday," he says. "Maybe Friday we could get together for a couple of hours in Washington on my way back to Paris." For this salesperson, a nice order is one with nine zeros after the number—as in *billions* of dollars.

John Leahy heads the global sales division of Airbus Industrie, the builder of jetliners that has, since its inception 20 years ago, become an industry leader, second only to Boeing. Airbus Industrie is an international consortium of French, German, British, and Spanish aircraft manufacturers. "Individually, none of them was strong enough to compete on a global scale, but as a team they have done very well," says Leahy. "Teamwork is the key to selling aircraft. It takes many people working together to design and build aircraft, and it certainly takes many people working together to sell them!"

Most of Leahy's adult life has revolved around selling and aviation, so it is only natural that he has risen to the pinnacle of success by merging both interests. He first took flying lessons in 1973, then he went on to earn his commercial pilot's license and his instrument and multi-engine ratings, ultimately becoming an instrument flight instructor. Leahy married in 1973, while attending Columbia University. The early months of the marriage were hard on the young couple. Leahy stayed in New York City pursuing an MBA while his wife, Grace, worked on her doctorate in computer science 250 miles away at Syracuse University. He eventually transferred to the same school that Grace attended and got a job as the pilot of a twin-engine cargo plane.

Four nights a week he would work the graveyard shift, loading two tons of freight into an aging Beechcraft at 9:00 P.M. and then flying it to Chicago. At O'Hare Airport he would unload, reload, and refuel before flying back across the snow belt and over the Great Lakes to Syracuse, where he would arrive at dawn. Those long nights of flying alone in the creaking, unpressurized plane through dreadful weather taught him the patience, perseverance, and resourcefulness that would later make him successful.

Selling the Big Birds

When Leahy graduated in 1977, he was hired by Piper Aircraft. He used his flying experience and his financial background to develop sales training and business management courses for the Piper dealer network. John did well at Piper and progressed rapidly through the ranks, heading, successively, the advertising, product planning, and public relations departments. In the summer of 1984, the company promoted him to director of sales for the Eastern Hemisphere, in Geneva, Switzerland. "I was about to make the move," he recalls. "We had sold the car and had almost sold the house. Then I got an invitation to meet with Airbus in New York."

The European company had not been very successful in selling their aircraft to airlines in the United States. Boeing and McDonnell Douglas were entrenched in the

domestic market, and the American airlines were hesitant about dealing with a foreign company. The European salespeople reinforced the fact that they were not a domestic company, and Airbus was interested in having an American salesperson working for them. They offered John Leahy a job as a salesman just one week after their first meeting.

"When I began working for Airbus, the company had only one customer in the United States," he says. "It was Eastern Airlines and, unfortunately, they were not well respected at the time. Pan Am had signed a memorandum of understanding, but that was much less than a firm order." His primary task was to work on obtaining a formal order from Pan Am. The Airbus team was successful in this endeavor. The sale to Pan Am, one of the most prestigious names in the airline world at the time, was a major breakthrough. Having gained a toehold in the

American market, Airbus was ready to move on to other opportunities, but the European company was clearly the outsider in the close-knit U.S. airline fraternity.

In the world of sales it is known that the current vendor should always "help" the customer write the specifications when requests for proposals (RFPs) for additional orders are drawn up. Any good salesperson understands their competitor's products enough to know how they differ from their own models and can list a few of the features that make their products unique. When an RFP is drawn up, the current vendor can insert one of these unique features into the specifications, giving them an advantage over their competitors. An IBM typewriter salesperson, for example, could insert the requirement that the product must be made in the United States, a car salesman might have the customer request that any vehicles they order have steering column transmission shift, and a life insurance agent could specify that the company that is selected must be licensed in all 50 states and have a AA+ rating. Their competitors might have products that otherwise fully comply, but if they cannot meet this specification, it provides the established supplier, and the corporate buyer who is comfortable with that vendor, an opportunity to reject competitors.

John Leahy says he found out early in his Airbus career that he had to devise a different strategy for competing. "When you are the underdog, as Airbus was in most Boeing- or McDonnell Douglas–dominated North American carriers, you cannot run a traditional RFP sales campaign successfully. The big gorilla always wins."

The strategy he developed was more like a guerrilla insurgency than the customary full-frontal attack.

> I used middle management contacts within an airline and simply went in to introduce our company to them. Then I would reason with them and talk about how our new twin-jet was saving other carriers millions of dollars in operating

costs over the tri-jet they had used. "Why don't we do some studies for you, just so you will know where you stand," I would say. This non-threatening, no-obligation approach worked. Then we would do the same for the marketing people, the flight planning department, and the operations folks. Then in six months, I would deliver some very impressive studies to the management of several key departments. When I brought them together, they saw that the advantages of our equipment extended beyond their own department to benefit the entire airline. *Then* they were interested.

His competitors, meanwhile, were usually unaware that all of this was going on because the carrier was not formally planning to order aircraft. Leahy says that Boeing would occasionally hear that something was going on and they would call someone they knew in the airline, asking if the airline was looking to buy new narrow-body planes. They would be told, truthfully, that the carrier was not preparing RFPs.

Nine months later, Airbus would fly several of the carrier's senior executives to Europe and demonstrate its airplane. Then they would show the American carriers their studies and would show them the testimonials from dozens of carriers around the world saying how reliable and efficient their aircraft were. "Our maintenance people would describe the low maintenance costs of our aircraft," Leahy explains. "The airline studies team would show them how the cash flow analysis benefited their stockholders. Another team would discuss route planning, and so on. When you sell capital equipment this complex, there is no single person who makes the sale, it is a total team effort."

This is exactly the strategy Airbus followed with Northwest Airlines. By the time Northwest's management team left their base at Toulouse, France, they were almost convinced that they should purchase the Airbus aircraft. When they returned to the United States it did not take

Boeing long to find out what had happened, and they scrambled to offer their 737-300.

At the eleventh hour, the Northwest executives expressed concern about the untested service reliability of a European supplier such as Airbus. Leahy asked them what the worst thing that could happen was. As they pondered the question, he proposed a solution that would dispel the carrier's concern. "This was a 100-aircraft order—a $3 billion sale. I said, 'How about a 10/90 deal? If the first 10 airplanes we send you do not perform, we will find customers for them and you do not have to go through with the other 90.' That took away their remaining objections and they went with us for the order. Boeing was absolutely livid. They tried to buy the order back from Northwest, but there was virtually nothing they could do." As if his anecdote had been timed to coincide with what was going on outside, John points out the window of the airport lounge. "Look, there is one of Northwest's A320s taking off right now," he says proudly. "They have 50 so far and have ordered 16 of our wide-body A330 long-haul twins."

The Best Laid Plans . . .

Piedmont Airlines was a small regional carrier based in North Carolina. For most of its history the company had maintained a low profile, flying routes below or just beyond the Mason-Dixon line. After the Airline Deregulation Act of 1978, they began spreading their wings far beyond their traditional territory. John Leahy remembers when he came close to getting Piedmont as a customer. In the mid-eighties, Leahy went to Piedmont and talked to them about the Airbus wide-body twins. At the time, Piedmont was a very close Boeing customer, so close, in fact, that several Piedmont executives subsequently went to work for Boeing. At first they were not interested in the Airbus airplane, but over time, as the European company showed them the studies on their operation, they became intrigued, and the initial contacts developed into a full-scale sales campaign. Then at the moment Piedmont had told Airbus to expect their decision, the announcement was delayed.

> The Piedmont executives were constantly asking new questions of us, and on the new date that they had set for making a decision, we flew to North Carolina to answer them directly to their senior management decision-making team. "Is there anything else you want to put on the table?" one of them asked. We had already shaved our price to the last nickel, so they asked us to return at 4:30 that afternoon. I left that boardroom knowing that our technology was more modern, our equipment was better, and our price was right at, or even below, the best Boeing had offered. Our team could not have made a more professional presentation.
>
> What I did not know was that Bill Howard, Piedmont's chief, enjoyed a personal friendship with Boeing chairman Frank Schrontz that dated back to World War II. After I left that morning, Frank Schrontz himself flew to Winston-Salem, North Carolina, to handle Boeing's final presentation to Piedmont. A person in the room later told me that Schrontz told the airline executives, "You're comfortable with us. You have used our airplanes for years. Why would you want to risk spending hundreds of millions of dollars with a foreign vendor you do not know?"

Then the Boeing chairman dropped the bombshell. Leahy says Schrontz told the executives that he had come personally to tell them that Boeing wanted the order. He said that he was offering a $4 million discount on each aircraft if they had a deal by the time he left the room. He assured the executives that it was a one-time offer that would expire when the meeting ended.

Leahy's contact said the group was astounded at the Boeing chief's incentive. They asked him to wait outside so they could discuss the matter privately. One person asked if they should call Boeing's bluff and see if Airbus would match the offer, but the consensus was that Frank Schrontz was serious in his threat. As they discussed the merits of each aircraft, someone asked how many of the executives in the room thought that the Airbus was worth $4 million per airplane more than the Boeing 767. There were few hands raised. Boeing had won.

As Boeing's chairman was flying west toward Seattle, John Leahy was ushered into the boardroom and was given the bad news. "In hindsight, I must say that Schrontz impressed me with how he pulled that off at the last minute," he admits. "It was dramatic and, in this case, obviously effective. Sometimes you have to grab the ball yourself and run it across the goal line, and that is what he did." For whatever solace it may have provided, several Piedmont executives told Leahy that the Airbus presentations were superb. They told him that it was his proactive approach that had created the order for wide-body aircraft, something the company never would have dreamed of buying a few months earlier.

John Leahy also saw his proposals to other American carriers shot down. Although he lost the campaigns, he felt he got a little closer to a victory each time. United was a classic example. That was probably the toughest sale he ever made, and it took more than one attempt. Except for some McDonnell Douglas DC-10s, United was traditionally an all-Boeing airline. During an earlier buy-out attempt, Boeing had invested $750 million in United's stock to support the company's existing management. In fact, in the thirties, United Airlines, Boeing, and engine maker Pratt and Whitney were one company. Deep down inside United, people felt very comfortable with their way of doing business with Boeing. They were very rigid. Nobody ever got fired for buying Boeings.

Leahy remembers being invited, along with McDonnell Douglas and Boeing, to bid on wide-body twins. After months of negotiations and a hard-fought campaign, he lost that campaign when United became the launch customer for the Boeing 777. Once again, the dominant existing supplier had the inside track because they had the experience of knowing what was important to that customer.

Seeing so many of his sales proposals rejected, after many months of work on each one, would have left the average salesperson depressed, or worse. John Leahy possesses the ability to see things in the longer term. He knew his company's product was sound—even superior—technologically. He saw the advances in market share that Airbus was achieving in other global markets, so he believed in what he was proposing. He had the vision to think long term and the analytical skills to recognize that each proposal had come a little closer to a sale. These things gave him the motivation to continue with enthusiasm and discipline through those early years with Airbus.

Flying High

Even though he had lost several sales campaigns with United, John Leahy initiated another. "It seems so long ago that I first sat down with United and said, 'Let's talk about a replacement plan for your aging Boeing 727s.' They would always say, 'We'll get around to that.' But over time they became interested. They began saying, 'This may be a worthwhile discussion.' Then it became, 'This might be too good a deal to pass up.' Of course, at that point, they brought Boeing in, and Boeing fought tooth and nail over every statistic we showed."

Leahy cannot count the number of times he and his team went back and forth with discussions, meeting United's people in Chicago, San Francisco, New York, and Paris. It was a bitter fight. "Once when we were meeting with them in a restaurant, I got a call saying that someone had exerted pressure on engine builder General Electric. GE had just issued a statement that they would not offer their CFMI engine for the A320s we were proposing to United."

Industry watchers anticipated that Boeing would again prevail, but United Airlines shocked the aviation world with the announcement that they had decided to purchase 50 Airbus A320 passenger jets in a deal worth $2 billion. The years of competition and rejected proposals had paid off for Leahy and his team. They had won the big prize, and many more would follow.

Federal Express had, at one point, considered acquiring a fleet of used cargo jets at $30 million apiece. When they saw the logic in the proposal presented by Leahy's team of financial and maintenance gurus, however, they ordered 25 new Airbus A300 freighters at $75 million a copy.

Carl Icahn, TWA's ebullient chairman, personally negotiated TWA's order for 20 long-range wide-body A330s in a deal that took several months to complete. The airline became a launch customer for the A330 after John Leahy's team demonstrated the economic and performance benefits of replacing their aging Lockheed L1011s with new fuel-efficient aircraft. Although Carl Icahn was a difficult negotiator—he walked out on the transaction no less than three times before they finally concluded the deal—he proved to be a gracious host. At one point he stopped the discussions to have the entire negotiating team sample the first-class cuisine he was evaluating for TWA's transatlantic routes.

As more Airbus aircraft plied the U.S. skies, their reliability statistics became common knowledge among airline executives. The epithet "foreign built," which had hurt the consortium's early efforts, became less of a liability once the company revealed that Airbus aircraft use components built by 800 U.S. suppliers in 40 states, and that using these components had pumped $10 billion back to those companies since 1990. "Actually, every Airbus airplane that is built brings a return to U.S. industry that is at least equal to that of any of the European partners in the consortium," John points out.

Structuring Highly Complex Sales

Air Canada and their rival, Canadian Airlines, ordered Airbus jets, as did America West, Braniff, and American Airlines. Selling aircraft worth hundreds of millions of dollars involves more than the normal sales processes of making a presentation and writing the order. The transaction with Braniff, for example, was so complex that more than 50 separate documents and side letters were required to close the deal among four different parties. In the few years before its demise, Pan Am realized that its contract to purchase up to 50 Airbus A320s had cash value that the carrier desperately needed. They asked Airbus to help them market their prime delivery positions of the popular new aircraft in an attempt to raise cash.

In a highly complex transaction involving Braniff, Pan Am, International Aero Engines, GPA (an Irish aircraft lessor), and Airbus Industrie, the Pan Am contracts were to be assigned to GPA for lease to Braniff. After several weeks of almost around-the-clock negotiations in New York City the contracts were finally signed at three minutes before midnight on December 31st—just 180 seconds before key tax credits worth tens of millions of dollars would have expired. An exhausted but exhilarated John Leahy brought the champagne for a much-welcomed New Year's celebration among the parties.

Pan Am received its much-needed cash from GPA, which now owned rights to the unbuilt aircraft. GPA had a lease commitment from Braniff for 24 A320 passenger jets. Unfortunately for GPA, Braniff declared bankruptcy about a year later. Airbus had delivered only a few of the aircraft, and GPA again asked that John help re-market the remaining planes. His team worked with America West Airlines, and in another complex financial transaction, the original Pan Am aircraft finally found a home in Phoenix where they are today flying profitably for America West.

His Career Soars

As the victories in this battle for the skies of North America became more frequent, John Leahy's career climbed. The foot soldier salesman hired by Airbus in 1985 was promoted to vice president of sales for North America just three years later. Then it was senior vice president of sales in 1989, followed by president of North American operations. Instead of being the person on the spot who could confidently handle anything a customer threw at him, he had to train, manage, and motivate others.

Understanding a World of Cultural Differences

Zig Ziglar, one of the world's preeminent sales trainers, says that "outstanding sales professionals are picture painters." If so, then John Leahy became a master painter, carefully matching his sales and technical staff with the character of his customers. He also skillfully contended with the inherent cultural and attitude differences in communicating with the multinational members of the European consortium.

According to Leahy, understanding the culture of the person with whom you are dealing is critical. He believes that salespeople have to adapt to the cultural style of the environment in which they are trying to sell, whether domestically or overseas. To illustrate the difference between U.S. and European personalities and to show how important it is to tailor an approach to the particular culture, John relates an incident told to him by the CEO of one U.S. airline. The executive told Leahy that when they would be ordering aircraft, they would often tell the manufacturer that they wanted something built into the design. The Airbus engineers would get all excited and wave their arms and say, "That is impossible! It cannot be done. Absolutely not!" Then the Boeing people would very calmly say, "OK, we understand what you want. We will be happy to take it back and try to work everything out for you. Now, let's get on with the contract." Then a couple of weeks later, the Boeing people would come back and give the most eloquent, well-rehearsed reasons why they could not make the change. The Airbus folks, however, would come back and say, "Our technical people took this as a challenge and have worked day and night on it. Here is how they say we can fulfill your request."

He tells the story not so much to tout his company's products as to illustrate the importance of cultural differences and customer perception. "As to the customer's perception, we are probably the most willing of any aircraft builder to work out a customer's specific requirements, yet we had the reputation of being inflexible. The customer remembers the person saying, 'That is impossible' much longer than the fact that he came back two weeks later and said, 'We can do it.' You cannot change that initial perception. So one way I felt we could increase our winning percentage had nothing to do with airplanes, technology, or price. We just had to change our sales approach and—especially in the North American market—take more of a customer-oriented approach to selling. I told the Airbus team, 'Please don't go into the meeting and tell the customer that what they want is impossible!' "

Traits of an Excellent Salesperson

In 1994, Airbus promoted John to the corporate headquarters in Toulouse, France, as senior vice president, commercial of Airbus Industrie, GIE. As the chief commercial officer, overseeing all global sales and marketing functions, he directs a worldwide sales team of 350 people from 44 different countries.

Despite the enormous cultural differences in such a diverse sales force, he finds the attributes of the best salespeople are the same: empathy, ego drive, and above-average intelligence. "I put intelligence last for a reason," he points out, "because the first two will get you most of the way in." As a sales manager who "walks the walk and talks the talk" himself, he recognizes the challenges that keep salespeople from attaining their goals. "You have to get up every single morning and make something happen," he advises. "When you meet your prospective customers, you need to ask yourself, 'What is the other guy thinking?' You cannot charge right into the meeting and start your presentation. That is why I say the most important thing you need, to be really successful, to earn the big end-of-year bonus, is empathy. Even the specialists we bring in for their technical expertise have to be empathetic communicators. Otherwise, they can talk their way right out of a sale."

John Leahy stops momentarily to point out two Airbus aircraft as an American Airlines and an Air Canada jet taxi by. Then he returns to his favorite subject: selling. "To be a great salesperson you must be an impresario," he declares. "You must be able to make a presentation to several different people while balancing egos, the numbers, and the benefits that your proposed solution will bring them. You must be empathetic in addressing the concerns of each person there because you need them to support you at decision time, when you will not be in the room. At the end of your presentation, you don't have to expect an order, but your goal must be to be closer to the deal than when the meeting began."

His advice is based on selling airplanes because that has been his area of expertise. Yet his words are just as relevant for the salesperson selling chemicals, cars, or computers. He stresses that the sales professional will create the need and a feeling of urgency to satisfy that need according to *his* schedule, not the customer's.

If you went into a Mercedes showroom with your wife and young children, the good car salesperson is going to talk about the safety of a Mercedes, its reliability in bad weather, the benefits of its crash protection features, and so on. Even if you cannot afford the car, the salesperson will make you feel a need for his product. Nevertheless, he has not closed the deal unless he can persuade you that you *can* afford that car and that you can afford to get it now. Perhaps it is a lease plan that will make it affordable, or a long-term loan. Our salespeople focus on the importance of creating the need to act now. Some of our weakest salespeople are those who say, "I have sold them on the airplane, but they say the price is too high right now."

He explains that he relies heavily on his team leaders to attract good people to their unit. In fact, he describes team building among his sales force as one of his most important duties. With contracts ranging from $40 million for a single aircraft to several billion dollars for a fleet replacement, he cannot risk a single member of the 350-person sales force not being at peak performance every day. "I have to ensure that each of them stays focused on the gold ring," he says. "Motivating 350 professionals from 44 countries is quite a challenge. You cannot do that from a book with a few inspiring epigrams."

They must be proficient and confident enough to manage their sales responsibilities, he says, yet they also need to be aware that senior management is there if they really need help. When Leahy was a flight instructor preparing students for their commercial pilot's license, he would take them up and put them through some advanced maneuvers, like spins and lazy eights. Then he would give the student pilot the controls and say, "Now you do that." Often he would see a panic-stricken look on their face and they would say something like, "I can't do that. I could kill myself." Leahy would tell them that he wanted them to learn how to recover from a spin; otherwise, if they inadvertently got into that situation, then yes, they might kill themselves. He assured them, however, that he would not be asking them to try the procedure if he was not confident that they could handle it since he certainly had no intention of killing *himself*.

"My role at Airbus is similar," he says. "I am there to ensure that our sales team can control their selling situations and attain our goals, but I am always ready if they need me. I believe that a good sales manager steps in 5 percent of the time, whereas a mediocre sales manager intercedes 50 percent of the time. I find it really exciting to see a team of dynamic, aggressive, charging people who just love to sell."

Leahy says he considers Lee Iacocca to be the best salesperson he has ever seen. "Think about it," he muses. "He took a company with a very bad public image and sold the fact that they were innovative and had good products. Then he took the firm's employees who had a number-three mentality and made them believe they were number one. He sold his suppliers, the unions, even the U.S. Congress, and did exactly what I said all good salespeople need to do: he made something happen."

Thriving on Challenge

John Leahy has certainly made something happen in just 10 short years with Airbus Industrie. He has risen from a sales representative to the head of all sales and marketing operations in the world. He has been instrumental in making a company that was a foreign outsider into an industry leader that was tied with Boeing in 1994, earning a 47 percent market share of orders from U.S. carriers. "I get bored quickly," he admits. "When I started with Airbus, I was not planning to stay here for more than three or four years. Yet I love selling airplanes, and although Airbus was a difficult aircraft to sell back then, I became ever more fascinated. I thrive on challenges, so there was nothing more likely to kick my ego drive into high gear than to have some airline executive tell me, 'This airline never buys foreign airplanes.'"

He recalls his early days with the company, when his prime responsibility was to help conclude the Pan Am transaction. When the carrier finally signed with Airbus, Leahy helped organize an elegant black tie dinner at the Metropolitan Museum of Art for 50 Pan Am management staff and their spouses, complete with an orchestra and limousines to and from the event. When he went to his boss for authorization, he got word back not to exceed $50,000 since that was the entire annual budget for the U.S. office for that type of event. So he went back to them and asked how on earth they could exhaust the annual budget on the Pan Am dinner and have nothing left for when they sold to the next airline. Their response to that was that he should not worry because they only got orders about every five years. "*That*," says John Leahy, "was the most motivational thing that anybody ever said to me."

Ron Rush

Superstar Time Manager, Marketer, and Realtor

Ron Rush is like an automaton. He is constantly aware of his personal limitations, his progress toward his current goals, and even the value of one minute of his time. He uses two powerful tools, delegation and technology, to mold his operation into one of the country's most efficient, productive real estate sales organizations. Like several of the other superstars profiled in these pages, Rush's million dollar income today began almost by accident, as a part-time source of pocket money.

Ron's first career was in the U.S. Air Force. While serving as a 2nd Lieutenant at Wright-Patterson Air Force base near Dayton, Ohio, a friend talked him into getting his real estate license. "Frank Biggs told me, 'You know lots of people. You would be a natural at it.' So I thought, 'Well, it beats sitting around watching TV.' Back then, you could buy a nice home in Dayton for $12,000. With a VA mortgage you could own it with only $400 down." With the ink still wet on his license, Rush sold his first home, earning a $150 commission.

For several years Rush's focus was on his military service and on his growing family. He also concentrated on furthering his education, and as a result, real estate stayed a hobby to which he devoted little time. The Air Force promoted him several times, and along the way he earned an MBA from Duquesne University. In 1971, Rush was assigned to the Pentagon and moved to the northern Virginia suburbs of the nation's capital. "Until then, real estate had been just a fun thing to play around with," he says. After his transfer he first went with a small local broker. Then in 1979, upon returning from a four-year posting in Korea, he joined Long & Foster, one of the country's largest independent real estate firms. Ron decided to pay more attention to the business.

The Beginning of a Career

Indeed he did. Ron Rush devoted an average of two hours each evening, and some weekends, to building his business. According to him, two things accounted for his early success. "At the University of Pittsburgh, they had spent lots of time drumming in the concept of time management, which at that point was a new idea," he says. "I came to realize that time management is the very essence of the real estate business. The other thing that helped was that I was a joiner. I was in everything. I attended my kids' sporting events, even coaching some of them. As I participated in these activities, more and more people came to know me as 'the real estate man.'"

In his first year as a part-time agent with Long & Foster, Ron Rush did $1 million in sales—and this was in the seventies. Each year his volume increased, and in 1981 he became the top-selling agent out of the 3,000 in the company. "It was kind of embarrassing for Wes Foster, the president of Long & Foster, to tell all the other agents that the top salesperson was a part-timer," he laughs.

Investing in a Support Staff

In 1981, as his real estate practice expanded, he retired from the Air Force as a lieutenant colonel. Now it was time to devote his full attention to what had become a very lucrative pastime. "The first year I went full-time in

real estate I did $11 million in sales," he says. "Then I floundered. My volume, my whole career, just hit a plateau. I knew what to do and how to do it, but I guess it was just a case of not knowing how to productively use all those daytime hours I suddenly had open." Many real estate agents would be very pleased with $11 million in annual sales *today,* let alone 13 years ago, but Rush knew he was in a rut and had to find a way out. To see what was keeping him from increasing his productivity, he took a week and wrote down every single thing he did every day. This experience taught him to delegate, and he suddenly found that he had much more time for doing what he did best—selling real estate. "I got smart, Ron says, "I realized that the best use of my time was being directly in front of buyers and sellers, not in the office typing contracts and ordering termite inspections. So I hired a part-time assistant." Initially his daughter Darlene helped him over the summer, and then he hired an office secretary. That year, his volume rose from $11 million to $17 million. Ron Rush was out of his rut.

As his practice grew, he expanded his support staff. The next year, sales rose to $25 million and Ron hired two more people, including his son, Mike. As the numbers continued to climb—$37 million in 1988 and $42 million in 1989—so did the number of administrative details. To cope with the paperwork and the logistical demands created by such enormous volume, he again increased his staff. By 1990, number of people working in his office was up to nine.

Sharing His Secrets to Success

Rush's superstar sales status had, by then, become known far beyond the Long & Foster network. The spotlight beckoned. "From time to time I had been asked to speak to groups of Realtors about my road to success. Most of the professional trainers I saw out there talked about what other people did. They had little or no real estate selling experience themselves. I felt as if I needed a break anyway, so when people asked me to go out on the lecture circuit, it seemed like a good idea."

For the next two years, Rush's days were spent in front of audiences around the country who came to hear the techniques and methods that had made him one of the industry's top producers. He made, and sold, a 14-hour audio tape series, and for a while he basked in the glow of the accolades and ovations from his peers. During the years of speaking to 25,000 people annually in distant cities, however, his own practice started a precipitous decline.

There is a Spanish proverb, *Las huelgas del agricola son el mejor abono,* that translates to "The footsteps of the farmer are the best manure." In Ron Rush's case, he was the farmer. None of his support staff were responsible for bringing in business. It is hardly surprising that while those two years as an industry celebrity were good for his frequent flyer account, they were nearly disastrous for his bank account. "My production went from the record $42 million to just over $12 million," he admits. He was getting tired of the incessant travel, and as he fulfilled his remaining speaking commitments, he pondered the impact that his lecturing had had on his real estate business. "Then in the winter of 1992, I got stranded by a snowstorm in Chicago," he recalls. "For two days I was stuck in a hotel room and I asked myself, 'Do I need this nonsense? I can make $5,000 a day selling real estate and that is exactly what I should be doing.' I realized that I needed to treat real estate and public speaking as separate businesses, and that's what I did. Now if a company calls me and asks me to come out and talk to their agents, the fee I charge is the amount of income I will lose from being away from my business."

Rebuilding His Business

It was quite a blow for Ron to return to his practice and see how much business he had lost. Several employees had to be let go, but because personal computers and software had dropped in price, Ron was able to computerize the office and the remaining staff was able to increase their productivity. "Computers have been a godsend to me," he says sincerely. "Still, with the reduced sales and support staff, I really had to go back to basics. I did things I had not done for years. I held open houses, made cold calls, and went out into my farm [his primary marketing area] to meet people."

In hindsight, the relative tranquillity of his office may have been a good thing. It gave Ron the time to re-engineer his entire operation, something he would never have envisioned had he been handling 300 transactions and $50 million in sales that year. He focused primarily on marketing and delegating the workload. Today his seven assistants have clearly defined roles, and Ron empowers them to make whatever decisions it takes to accomplish their objectives.

Rush calculated his annual income and broke that down to an hourly figure. "My charge rate is between $500 and $600 per hour," he says. "That is how much I earn by being in front of a client, say, at a listing appointment. Every time I'm faced with an activity, I have to ask myself, 'Will this task earn me more than my charge rate?' Take, for example, writing a letter. If it will not earn me more than that rate, I get someone else to do it." He is amazed by how many agents who have thriving, successful practices undertake time-wasting chores such as writing advertisements, taking photographs of their listings, or driving around putting up signs.

Developing a Marketing Machine

Ron Rush's greatest change has been his aggressive marketing campaign. Although he is an agent housed in Long & Foster's Fair Oaks office in Fairfax, Virginia, he is a de facto company within a company. Dedicated telephone lines ring directly to his staff, and he directs his own marketing. He makes extensive use of desktop publishing and places heavy emphasis on personal marketing. His name and photograph appear on his letterhead, business cards, and brochures. Every time one of his listings sells, his staff mails out 1,000 "Just Sold" cards emblazoned with "Ron Did it Again!" to the surrounding neighborhood. Other direct mail pieces display catch phrases such as "Run to Ron when you need real estate" below his omnipresent picture.

Rush sends two or three mailing pieces each month to his entire 50,000-name farm area, and he also sends his own monthly newsletter to prospective, present, and past clients. "I want to maintain a personal relationship with people," he says. "I have had other agents say, 'I do not advertise,' and that's all right for them. You have to do what is comfortable for you. When I made number one at Long & Foster, I mailed out 100,000 flyers announcing the fact."

Do the results justify the production and mailing costs of this year-round campaign? "You bet it does," he answers. "I get incredible results from my direct mail. I have even received calls from people in California asking me to list their homes here." He has had total strangers approach him, saying, "Hey! You're Ron Rush, the real estate guy," which validates his reasons for using his photograph on all of his marketing pieces.

The second phase of Rush's marketing program is his telemarketing operation. Five evenings a week a professionally trained three-person telemarketing staff calls 500 people in his marketing area. That is 2,500 people every single week that are asked whether they are planning to buy or sell a home, or if they have a friend or relative who is. The crew also calls homeowners in the neighborhoods where Rush has recently sold a house, telling them that he had other buyers who were interested in the neighborhood. That is sometimes all that is necessary to prompt homeowners to put their house on the market.

"This is a way I can clone myself and make more calls," he explains. The telemarketing program reaches an enormous number of potential customers, and the relevant notes from every call go into a report that Ron receives the next morning.

After he reviews the report, remarks about the call, such as that the owners are planning to sell their house in six months, are entered into his database for an automatic reminder in five months. Rush calls this "banking prospects for future sales" and says he has more than 1,500 future listing appointments stored in the system for follow-up.

The Work Ethic Pays Big Dividends

The re-engineered Ron Rush constantly evaluates himself and his operation for maximum efficiency. "My strength is that I have a system," he says. "I even buy gas on my way home at 11:00 P.M. because there are no lines then. I am up every day at 6:00 A.M., and I am in the office by 6:30." By 9:00 A.M. he has reviewed the multiple listing service (MLS) computer printout of other brokers' listings which expired at midnight, and has called those homeowners whose listings he would like to pick up.

His staff monitors all incoming calls; getting through directly to Ron Rush by telephone is impossible. When a person calls his office, his employees usually transfer the call to the staff member handling the matter in question. If a client insists on speaking with Ron personally, the employee discovers why and then passes the message on to him. This procedure ensures that his current activity is not interrupted, and it gives him the opportunity to investigate the topic of the caller's question.

When Ron Rush leaves for a listing appointment, his staff hands him a customized listing presentation package, complete with a printout of all the comparable properties in the neighborhood that are currently for sale or have recently sold. All he has to do is glance over their work before arriving at the appointment. Many Realtors typically take two hours on an initial listing presentation and then return for another hour or so a few days later after the prospect has had a chance to read their package. Ron Rush's listing appointments are done in one visit that usually lasts 20–30 minutes. His strategy is to always schedule himself as the last agent in. "That way," he explains, "I know against whom I am competing." He says he successfully closes 96 percent of his listing presentations.

One might surmise that a Realtor doing $40 million in sales must attain such figures by selling million dollar homes. Not so with Ron Rush. His biggest sale ever was $540,000, and he averages transactions in the low $200,000 range. The sales that give him the greatest satisfaction are those to first-time home buyers. "They are so proud and happy at settlement," he smiles. "When they get the keys they cry and hug me. Often those are the customers for whom I have interceded with the mortgage vendor because of a blemish on their credit history. Seeing customers so happy still gives me a real charge."

Overcoming Problems and Disappointments

Not all of Rush's transactions end with smiles.

> I have the worst situation in my entire career going on right now. A really nice customer bought a new-construction home through me. It was supposed to close in July, and here we are in October and the house is not finished. What is worse, the builder has been awful. Everything in the world has been wrong: the basement door is in the wrong place, the pantry is wrong, and one wall is six inches from where it is supposed to be. The builder also completely forgot to build the garage. Now, because of the delays, the buyer's financing package has fallen through and the current interest rates are much higher than the one he got when he bought the house. The buyer has wanted to walk away from it about 10 times.

Rush says such situations call for creativity, a proactive approach with the buyer and builder, and above all, the resourcefulness to keep both sides calm. "I never let any-thing that is a problem get to me," he adds. "You can't. If you did, it would grow like a cancer and destroy you."

A case in point is the situation that was, according to Ron, the toughest loss he ever had. The day before settle-ment, the lender rejected a buyer of one of his listings. Meanwhile, his client, the seller, had already moved to a rental home because their new house was not ready. He subsequently discovered that the buyer had a marginal credit rating all along—a point never revealed by his agent. "You take even the bad things and turn them into learning experiences," he philosophizes. "This taught me that I can make things happen when I control them. Never again have I taken an agent's word that the mortgage is approved."

When he experiences a setback, he says, the most important thing is not to take the loss so seriously that it leads to depression. He analyzes the situation, figures out why the loss occurred, and learns what he should do better next time. "I need to discover whether I lost it because the listing went to a friend in the business, or if I lost it because the other agent built a better mousetrap," he says. "I would not be able to sleep without knowing that."

He may have an occasional disappointment, but Ron says it never affects him to the point where he feels down. "I simply do not let it happen," he claims. "I will not let stress get inside me. I train myself to not see things as problems, only as opportunities to resolve."

Salespeople Who Thrive on Mediocrity

Ron Rush met thousands of Realtors on his seminar tours, and has encountered hundreds of others who sell his list-ings. Through his experience with so many agents he has formed some strong opinions on what prevents so many of them from becoming top producers. He believes that most agents are afraid to be successful and that the gap between good agents and those who play around in the real estate business is widening. He feels that in the future there will be fewer small agents and a much larger market share will go to the top producers.

> Look, I know one agency that has 85 agents in their office. There are five top-flight producers and another three or four mid-range agents who have potential. The others are breathing air, taking up space, barely getting by—and they're satisfied with that. That is fairly typical for this business. There are doers and do-notters. I saw it every day when I spoke to groups of agents around the country. Out of the 500 people that would show up at a seminar, 10 or 15 would buy self-improvement tapes and books sight unseen. The next 25 would think about it. The other 450 would come near, but would not even touch the tapes because it might make them feel committed. Sometimes I think their rationale is, "I don't want to have more sales, because then I would make more money, and then I would have tax problems."

> I saw many people taking tons of notes every time I spoke, but I know that when they returned to their offices, the notes got stuffed in a file drawer, never to be seen again. It does not matter how many success secrets I shared with them; within one week they would be acting exactly as they were before. I can change the lives of maybe 20 people in the room and help them make more money. The others will just continue along their paths to mediocrity.

What about the challenge of balancing his time between family and business? "Real estate is *my* life," he replies. "I can't ever turn it totally off. It's always there. I schedule time with my grown children and time to play golf. I travel and I make time to take my grandchildren out. I also spend personal quality time with my mom, who recently moved from Pittsburgh to be near me. I am happy with what I do."

Advice for Other Agents

In 1995, about 10 percent of Rush's business, more than $4 million in sales, will come from homes that were originally advertised as For Sale by Owner (FSBO). He freely shares advice on this topic with other agents. Many brokers go after FSBOs with the attitude that the owners are never going to sell the house by themselves. Rush explains that this immediately creates a confrontational barrier between the seller and the Realtor. "I let the FSBO know I'm going to *help* them," he says. He gives them a three-hour tape that has dozens of tips on how to sell the house. Then he follows up with a phone call once a week to answer questions and to update them on market conditions. Often after a few weeks of unannounced strangers walking through their home at all hours, the seller will call Rush in, saying, "I had no idea how complicated this was. Please list me!" Even when the homeowner does make a direct sale, they often tell their neighbors how great Rush was. He says that either way, he wins. "Why would you want to alienate that guy by telling him FSBOs do not know what they are doing and are totally wrong?" he ponders.

Some salespeople complain that their competitors lack professional selling skills and that they resort to cutting their price to win the business. Ron occasionally encounters them, too, but cautions salespeople not to be intimidated by their tactics. "Commission controls service," he explains. "On any given day there are 12,450 listings in our local MLS system. As many as 200 new—competing—properties come on the market every day. I spend $150,000 of my own money promoting my listings each year. If you list with someone whose discounted commission precludes advertising it effectively, you are not going to get the full value for your home. If you are not getting the full sales price, what difference does a lower commission make?"

Perhaps Ron Rush's most valuable bit of advice is his credo of customer service. He says the most frequent complaint he hears about other Realtors is that the client never hears from them once they sign the listing contract. "By the time the seller gets really steamed and calls their office, they are told that the agent is off that day, or is on vacation." Ron maintains that the most important single act of good service to a customer is regular communication so they know what is going on with the marketing of their property. "I tell my clients there is a number right on my business card where they can call me 24 hours a day," he says. "I receive about 200 calls a day from customers. If they have a problem or a question that my support staff cannot handle for them, they know I will be returning their call personally, every single time."

Moving the Goalposts

It has been an interesting second career for the Air Force officer who dabbled in real estate for a little spare cash those many years ago. He has seen the peaks of accomplishment that set him apart as one of the top real estate agents in the country. Nevertheless, he has also encountered the same barriers to success that many good sales professionals face. He has deviated from his specialty, has gotten stuck on a sales plateau, and has even had to rebuild his practice almost from the ground up. What sets Ron Rush apart is that he recognized the warning signs, evaluated his options, and changed course to prevent the barriers from becoming insurmountable roadblocks.

Today Ron Rush is a true sales superstar. Less than two years after returning from the speaking circuit to discover his business had plummeted to $12 million annually, he ended 1994 with more than $36 million in sales from 186 transactions. That is a $10 million increase from 1993. His marketing campaign is unparalleled in the industry, and he sets goals and measures his performance on a daily basis. "In real estate, as in life," he says, "you can become anything you want. I really love what I do. My personal credo is that there is absolutely nothing I won't do to ensure that my customers are satisfied. Once an offer comes in, I will fight tooth and nail, doing whatever it takes to put—and keep—a deal together. My dedication to the real estate profession is total, and the business has given a lot to me in return. But I will go to the end of the earth for a customer."

Ron Rush has shown that he has the creativity and drive to do whatever it takes to be a superstar salesperson. Sure, he works long hours, but that is a choice he makes in order to build his business. While others may want to get home in time for a favorite television show each evening, Ron chooses to use those precious minutes on a listing appointment. More importantly, Ron has designed a way to maximize the way he spends his time, delegating those tasks which so many of us take on to the detriment of our own productivity. He learns from his mistakes, operates a personal marketing program that is a major client-building asset, and simply loves selling real estate.

So where does he go from here? "I want to continue growing," he answers. "I would like to do $70 million, maybe even $100 million in a couple of years . . ." *One hundred million dollars?* Can one residential real estate salesperson selling $225,000 homes really expect to reach such a goal? "I'm not just any agent," he says. "I'm sorry, but in this business you can't be a humble introvert. Look at my numbers now, compared with those of the MLS agents against whom I compete. Their average home sells for 3–5 percent below listing price, mine average 1–2 percent. Their average home sells in 87 days. Mine sell in 32 days. All I know is that I have the system, the support staff, and the drive to achieve my goals. You can bet I'm going to put forth the best effort I can muster."

It is time to go. It is 11:00 A.M., and Ron Rush has to give his staff the two new listings he picked up on the way to the office this morning. While we were talking, other brokers faxed offers in on two of his current listings. It is time to take the good news to his customers.

Tom Stormer

★

Digital's Steeltown Superstar

If you subscribe to the adage that first impressions count, you are going to like Tom Stormer. He is not your typical big computer company salesperson type, but comes across as a very knowledgeable, likable guy. You feel happy when the receptionist announces that he is here to see you. You never feel as if he is trying to sell you something, but you know that he can probably design a solution for any high-tech problem you have.

Tom Stormer has lived all of his 40 years in the coal mining and steel mill region near Pittsburgh, Pennsylvania. Comedians called Pittsburgh "the only city you can smell before you can see." The city's image began to change in the seventies when environmental legislation and a shift in the industrial base transformed the entire area. Today Pittsburgh is a glittering city, home to some of America's most prestigious corporate headquarters. Its service- and technology-based industries drive a vibrant regional economy.

Stormer's life has mirrored the development of the region. "The good part of growing up in a middle-class family in this area was that they instilled in me a strong work ethic," says Tom today. "I pretty much coasted through high school, finishing in the bottom 10 percent of my class. Then something happened. I suddenly realized

155

what my future as a coal miner or steel mill employee would be like. I thought, 'This is my life? Being a mule for some company, spending every working moment in dirt and grime?' I realized that my grades and skills were not going to enable me to work any place else and that I could, no, I *must* change myself." Tom earned admission to college, and the transformation took him from the bottom of the class in high school to the top of the class in college.

"I didn't know what I wanted to do," he admits, "but the last thing I aspired to be was a salesperson. In the environment from which I came, the very word 'salesman' connoted deceit and distrust. My whole family was honest to a fault, and my parents instilled values in me that guide my decisions to this day."

A Career in Sales

After Stormer graduated in 1975, the Burroughs Corporation offered him an entry-level sales position. Despite the anticipated negative response from his family, Stormer decided that sales success and high ethical standards were not mutually exclusive.

The mid-seventies saw the dawning of the computer age. In the earlier part of the decade, long before there were personal computers on every desk, electronic calculators began replacing ancient adding machines and slide rules. Burroughs was on the leading edge of this technology, and they assigned Tom Stormer to sell these machines in the western Pennsylvania area. He focused his sales efforts primarily on the banking industry. He discovered quite early in his career that by specializing in a vertical market he could use the solutions he designed for one client in his marketing approach to the next prospect in the same industry. He did so well that Burroughs promoted him three times in the first four years.

Within three years of starting with the company, Stormer moved into sales management. He was still a salesman, but he now had the additional responsibility of

overseeing other salespeople. "I chose to make our unit a team rather than use the traditional sales manager/sales representative hierarchical model," he says today. "Our goal was to do nothing less than destroy the competition. I have always been fairly aggressive and focused, so that helped me in the serious part of my duties. Then I made a game out of our mission so we all had fun. It worked! We did smash the competition and everybody won in the process." Burroughs merged with Sperry Corporation, which had recently taken over computer giant Univac.

The Next Step

The shuffling and realignments at the corporate level, and the downsizing that affected his own branch, made Tom feel the company was not positioning itself to take advantage of the impending PC revolution. In 1988, he moved to Digital Corporation, the company where he continues to work today.

Some people may have considered the move from sales manager to sales representative a step back, but he says he never cared much about titles. "You have to look beyond the titles and when I did, I saw a company perfectly positioned for long-term success in the technology market." Digital was the second largest computer company in the world, and while being a sales manager was fun and rewarding, Stormer really loved selling. Digital gave him an opportunity to do that again full-time.

Tom Stormer has always liked dealing with large accounts. When he began working for Digital he was assigned to several Fortune 500 customers in western Pennsylvania. As he became more successful, he concentrated only on those in the city of Pittsburgh. His sales success was both remarkable and consistent. In his first year with Digital he received the DEC 100 Award for exceeding his annual goals, and has received it in every one of the eight years since. He has also won the Decathlon Award, the highest sales award in the company, and four times he has ranked among Digital's top 700 salespeople worldwide, each time earning an all-expenses-paid trip to Hawaii. He consistently places at or near the top of all salespeople in the industry.

"I treat my job as if I were on straight commission," he says. "That helps me to hit the ground running every morning. I am always very conscious of never losing my competitive spirit, that urge to win that I carry inside me." This attitude of treating his job as if his income depended on making every sale has paid off. "They have rewarded me with some quite amazing bonuses," he reveals, illustrating that in the end, his commission approach proved realistic.

Specializing in a Market Niche

Tom achieved considerable success by selling to the financial services industry, and he continues to concentrate his marketing efforts on that niche today. One of the reasons he has been so successful is that he sees himself not as a computer salesperson, but as someone who can create solutions for anything that uses technology. He recalls one sales success that shows how he made a huge sale by looking beyond his company's products, changing the paradigm that he and his peers had traditionally used.

He had been calling on a bank and had not done much business with them, but knew the potential was there. While waiting to see someone in the bank one day, Stormer noticed boxes of personal computers all over the place. He counted them and did a quick calculation. He estimated that they were worth about $400,000. After asking a few questions, Stormer discovered that people in that bank were buying more than $1 million worth of PCs a year, and nobody in central purchasing knew about it!

As he talked to the employees and looked more carefully at the boxes, he found that there was no commonality, control, or insight in their conversion to desktop computers. The buying decisions were disjointed. Most of the end users did not have a clue about what to order, nor how to use them. The only problem was, Digital was not competitive with PCs at the time, so Stormer had no product that he could sell them.

Many salespeople would not have even noticed the computer cartons lying around in the first place. Others might have noticed the delivery, but would have considered themselves too late to try to make a sale. Most sales representatives, realizing that they had no comparable competitive product, would never have pursued the matter. Sales superstars, however, have an innate sense for detecting opportunities, and Tom Stormer is a superstar.

He realized there was no vision of their computerization goals here, no procurement strategy. He wondered how he could address this for the executives who would be using the PCs, and tried to come up with a solution to their computerization problems. He asked one of his contacts at the bank about the computers. He was told how the bank employees were ordering different brands and models of hardware. Then there was the software nightmare which they had not even addressed yet. "So I designed a single-source solution for them," Stormer says. "I said, 'Bring it all to Mother Digital. I will deal with each secretary and manager, discover their needs, and supply the right hardware and software. I will even walk them through the installation and establish a network so they can all communicate with each other. Furthermore, if they ever have a problem, no matter what the brand of computer, and regardless of whether it is with their PC, software, or printer, they will have one person to call for help.' "

Since Digital did not manufacture most of the hardware, Stormer purchased the computers from vendors such as AST and Toshiba, adding a reasonable markup to their wholesale cost. By looking "outside the box" and seeing the end result instead of the barrier, Tom Stormer discovered a new market niche of multimillion-dollar bank customers, and his innovative solution made a valuable contribution to his company's bottom line.

Finding Solutions Can Create Sales

As the banking industry began to computerize, Tom Stormer led the charge of the salespeople selling them the needed technology. "The competition has become really intense," he says. "Still, I have won orders 14 consecutive times against my rivals from IBM and NCR." When he was not preparing a bid against his blue-chip competitors for the business of the big financial institutions, he was developing strategies to break into the smaller banks overlooked by his adversaries. Tom is especially proud of one such project. He brought together a group of tiny, independent, non-competing banks and proposed that they form a joint data processing consortium.

> There have been so many mergers and acquisitions in the banking business that the small community banks are having a hard time staying competitive. The larger regional banks have enormous in-house banking services that are made possible by very sophisticated computers that the little two-branch hometown banks cannot afford. I structured a deal where the smaller banks could pool their resources and jointly own a state-of-the-art system to rapidly and efficiently provide the same services for their customers as the giant banks offered. It had never been done before at Digital, but they went for it. It resulted in a sale of more than $5 million for me, and I used it as the prototype to pattern many subsequent proposals. It really was a mutually beneficial solution. Everybody won—the banks, their customers, Digital, and me.

The company sent his imaginative plan to other Digital branches, and according to Stormer, that idea has resulted in millions of dollars in sales nationwide. Tom Stormer had again looked beyond the barrier—the small banks' inability to buy—and had envisioned a solution that resulted in a substantial sale. "My competitor could not do it," he observes. "I identified the critical issue and got the competitive advantage."

Overcoming the Lost Sale Blues

Like all salespeople, superstars sometimes lose a sale. When that happens to Tom, he takes the loss very hard—but only for a short while. "My philosophy is, I'm not authorized to lose," he laughs. "I know it is my responsibility to present the proposal to the customer so that we both win."

Yet occasionally, things go wrong. Stormer recently had a situation where a competitor came in 50 percent below his price. He used all his skills, but could not overcome that price difference. "It was only a million-dollar contract," he explains, "but I really wanted it. I overcame many objections, but could not come close on the price." He admits he was in a daze when he left the customer, knowing he had lost the sale. Stormer drove through a red light, then drove the wrong way down a one-way street and got a ticket. He overcame the disappointment by totally immersing himself in his work. Within three days he had replaced that business with new orders and was out of his rut.

What did he learn from the lost sale? He says it taught him that customers are unpredictable; many executives in the firm had told him that he had the order. He also realized that sales professionals should never count on the business until the order is consummated. "Another lesson I learned was that to a customer, perception is reality," he explains. "I knew that, technologically, they were making a big mistake in buying the other equipment. However, they did not base the order on scientific, quantifiable reality. The customer perceived it as a good deal, and therefore I was out of the picture." Suddenly, the affable Tom Stormer's features tighten and he points his finger at his imagined competitor. "Still, I'm telling you," he says firmly, "now that I know how you sell, I'm coming after you. You may have won that order, that little battle, but mark my words, I will win the war!"

Observing Other Salespeople

As a sales manager at Burroughs and as a mentor to many salespeople at Digital, Tom Stormer has had the opportunity to observe many sales representatives from various industries. He has seen their strengths and weaknesses, and he has formed opinions about what keeps them from succeeding. He believes salespeople's biggest barrier to success is their inconsistency. "They might win a nice order and then coast for a month. You cannot do that," he says.

"I work with the same intensity whether I am at 10 percent or 200 percent of my goal. That's one reason I win more than 90 percent of all my proposals." Yet he warns that even if you have won the last 10 deals, you cannot consider yourself invincible. You have to be a little paranoid. "That keeps me alert when I'm in the customer's office," he says, "and it gives me a mental edge." Above all, Stormer says, salespeople cannot assume they will be successful just because they know all about their product. You have to sell *yourself* to the customer first.

Stormer believes the best salesperson he has ever seen is Tom Hempfield, a fellow Digital employee. Whenever Stormer worked with a sales rep, he would put them to a little mental test. After working with them for a while, he would ask himself, "If I were competing with this person, how often could he or she beat me? Two out of 10 times? Six out of 10?" If he figured on a number higher than five, he considered them true competitors. "Tom Hempfield is a great salesperson; he is honest, aggressive, and creative. When I first worked with Tom I thought, 'This guy scares me! I don't know that I could beat him.' "

Focusing on the Priorities

What are the roadblocks that prevent Tom Stormer from reaching an even higher level? "As driven as I am to achieve and exceed every goal the company throws at me, I have found I can lose focus on the real priorities of my life," he says thoughtfully. "You go out every day and win battles, blow away the competition, and hear customers tell you how great you are. It's easy to think you can control too much. Then you lose track of the things that are really important to you."

Stormer says that he overcomes this hurdle by maintaining a positive attitude and believing that it is his job to design a specific solution for each customer. "If you can understand what the customer wants, you can win," he adds. "Even if you have to suggest a competitor's product, you have won the customer's respect." Tom recalls an occasion when he did exactly that. He ranked the products of each vendor his customer had invited to bid. It so startled the client to see that Tom had placed a competitor's product higher than Digital's in a couple of categories that he awarded the business to Tom anyway. "What a learning experience that was! You see, honesty *does* pay," he says with a smile.

Despite his accomplishments, Stormer maintains an active life outside the sales arena and is fiercely protective of the time he spends with his family, his faith, and his friends at home. He volunteers at his church's school and makes sure he allows special, private time with each of his children, aged 22, 18, 16, and 14. He also has a project where he collects old computers, refurbishes and updates them to today's standards, and then gives them to small schools and missionary groups.

Handling Rejection

How does he deal with the stalling tactics and the rejection that salespeople must endure every day? "First, you should be grown-up enough to know that you do not always win every one," he answers. He admits that there was a point in his career when he believed he could, but that he had been brainwashed. "I know rejection hurts," he cautions, "but you are always going to have some rejection, so you just need to figure out the right amount. There are times when you can treat it aggressively, like when you have designed the best solution and the numbers are right, but you suspect the purchasing agent is giving the business to a friend who has an inferior product." In a case like that, Stormer says he would go right over the purchasing agent's head. "What do you have to lose?" he asks. "Just tell yourself, 'I am authorized to do this. Figures do not lie, and it is in this customer's best interest for them to use my solution.'"

As every salesperson knows, sometimes the prospect does not give you a hard target. Instead of saying, "No, we are buying from XYZ," they continually stall and delay the salesperson. How does Tom Stormer focus on a moving target like this?

> You have to find what makes that person tick. Figure it out yourself, or confidentially ask the advice of someone else in the company. Ask them, "Why does he keep putting me off? Is he lazy? Is one of my competitors a friend of his? Is he waiting for budget approval?" Use your brain and find out why you're getting stalled. If I have a viable solution and my numbers are good, this person cannot stop me. Now, if I can prove the dollars and cents, I win. Often the purchasing agent is overworked and under-recognized, so the most natural person for them to take it out on is the sales rep who comes calling. Before I give up on that decision maker and go over his or her head, I will take any nugget I can find and build him up. Take a part of the solution you have designed and give him ownership of it. It's amazing how a person like that will respond to you when you say, "That's a great idea! I really appreciate the suggestion. I owe you lunch."

Putting Himself in the Customer's Shoes

Tom Stormer loves the mental challenges that lead to sales success. When he first talks to a prospect that could potentially give him business, he says he lets his mind become that person. He finds out as much as he can about the company, its culture, their buying habits, and their needs, and does the same with the individual who has the buying authority. He explains that in his mind he becomes that person. He feels the essence of that buyer doing their job. He tries to imagine what their goals and fears are, where their stresses come from, and what they will feel like after they install his product. "You see," he says, "once I role play like that, I become the essence of what I'm trying to create. If I understand what their problems are, I can design a solution with which they will agree." Stormer describes this as his pathway to success, while his competitor is sitting there saying to the customer, in effect, "Why can't you understand what I am trying to sell you?"

These mind games have been the hallmark of Stormer's considerable success in the selling profession. Some would call his style "empathetic selling." Others would describe it as "customer-first relationships" or "non-manipulative selling." Whatever the label, his sales techniques come right out of the textbook from Marketing 101. He first finds out what the customer needs and then provides a solution to those needs. There is no mystique in it and it sounds so simple that no one would ever buy the book or pay to attend a seminar on his selling skills to learn it. The question that goes unanswered is, if it is so obvious, why do so many salespeople fail to follow this method?

Before you memorize Tom's lines and go charging off to make your next sales calls as the Reborn Salesperson, beware! Tom Stormer does not simply recite a few memorized lines of engaging repartee. What he says comes from the innermost element of his soul. Stormer really *wants* to solve a client's problems. If you listen to him talk about his work, you never hear him bring up the sales he made. Instead, you hear him get visibly excited when he discusses the solutions he designed for one company, or when he tells how another firm's CEO so appreciated his help that he called Stormer their most valuable employee, although he is, of course, not on their payroll.

Bob Russell, Digital's vice president for the financial services market, says of him, "We have consistently challenged Tom with the largest sales budget within the branch, yet he has significantly overachieved each year. For example, although we assigned him a very large increase for his 1994 goal, he finished the year at 255 percent of his target. His clients trust and respect his input because he places their needs first. His focus on their business problem is second to none. He will not relent once he has identified a proposed solution."

"I'm not a smooth, sweet-talking guy," this likable, slightly rumpled superstar says, almost apologetically. "However, I am brutally honest, I am reliable and consistent, I love being creative, and I will work for my customers until I drop." The interview is over. Digital's top salesperson has an appointment with a large prospective customer.

"I just thought of something I would like to say," he adds. "Do you know why I win? Because after I have psychologically put myself in the buyer's place, after I have designed a solution and shown them it is the only solution that makes sense and justifies the numbers, I make it fun. I take some of the most complex matters in business—buying computers and high-tech products—and make them simple. My customers love to give me orders because I make it easy for them to buy."

Frank Pacetta

★

Getting Them All Fired Up at Xerox

Frank Pacetta. At first glance, he looks like a management type from one of America's blue-chip companies: white shirt, silk tie, well-tailored suit, and gleaming shoes. Yet when he talks about the challenges confronting salespeople in the real world today, the metaphors he uses suggest a military background.

If anyone has the right to talk about how to develop sales superstars, it should be this man who was a college goof-off who stumbled into sales, then stumbled *along* in sales. Who, as a young man, finally listened to his dad's advice and became a salesman, then a really good salesman, then a district sales manager. Not just any sales manager, but one so effective that he was profiled on the front page of *The Wall Street Journal* after leading his team from last place in the company nationwide to first place. Yes, that seems like a person from whom the average sales rep could learn something. So what is it with the camouflaged army helmet on your desk, Frank?

"Because it's war out there," he declares. "Being in sales today is like being in the infantry. You study the territory, you learn how to use whatever weapons you have, then you walk right into battle. That's what it's like competing against an enemy who is trying to get their products into the customer at your expense. That's how it feels when you are on the front line making cold calls." As we discovered in the Gulf conflict, despite all of our technology and modern weaponry, we need the infantry to win the war. Pacetta's point is that in modern-day selling, the use of voice mail, fax machines, E-mail, and satellite communications will not win new customers, but an effective, properly trained, well-equipped sales team will.

"I credit my mom and dad for my sales success," he says. "The values they instilled in me as a teenager are what became the foundation for the type of manager I am today." He seems to echo Mark Twain when he admits that it took a few years for those values to sink in. That famous author once wrote, "When I was 14 years old, my father was so ignorant I could hardly stand to have the old man around. But when I got to be 21, I was astonished at how much the old man had learned in seven years."

A Mediocre Start to an Illustrious Career

After finishing high school, Frank left his hometown, Far Rockaway, New York, and studied at the University of Dayton, graduating with a degree in business. In 1976, a friend talked him into joining Xerox as a sales trainee. While some of the superstars profiled in this book soared to the top of their company's sales force in their very first year, Frank Pacetta's story is different. "I wanted to make some money and have fun," he says of his career goals at the time. "Nevertheless, I still clearly remember my first sale. It was a Xerox 660 desktop copier. That model must have weighed 300 pounds. I sold it to a doctor's office in Galion, Ohio, and I was so excited that I drove back to Columbus to turn in the order." He let the first three or four years of his career go by with mediocre sales, he admits, because he lacked dedication and organization.

Then he sold a big order of Xerox's 9200 models, their top-of-the-line copier at the time, and that year he was the top sales rep in the district. "In the midst of the

celebration, as I reflected on how good life was, my manager pulled me into his office," Pacetta recalls. "'Let me give you a little feedback,' he said. 'Despite this year's sales, you have not been performing up to your potential since you got here. You have more talent in your finger than anyone else in the office has in their entire body. You can go places in this company if you want to. The decision on whether this remains a job or becomes a career is up to you.' I decided right there to do something positive and to dedicate myself to building a career as a leader, a manager."

At Xerox, candidates for promotion are selected by a panel. When a sales manager's job opened, Frank applied for it and was interviewed by the panel, but was rejected. Some time later another vacancy became available, but the panel again declined his bid for the position. "I thought it was all their fault," he says today. "After all, my numbers were fabulous. So I sought my father's advice." The veteran Chase Manhattan Bank executive asked Frank what he had done differently on the second interview than he had on the first. "I told him that I had not changed a thing," he says. "Both interviews were basically the same."

His dad chastised him for his lack of foresight. He asked his son why, if the things he said and did on the first interview were not good enough to get him promoted, he would copy them a second time. "As usual," admits Pacetta, "my dad was right." The next time a promotion opportunity opened, he altered his presentation and was successful. It was time to get serious about his career with the Xerox Corporation.

Turning Lemons into Lemonade

From Columbus, Ohio, he moved to the office in Minneapolis, Minnesota, where, in 1987, he became the number one district sales manager in the country. Then he was offered a position that could make or break his career dreams with the company; he was asked if he would take the district manager's position in the Cleveland sales office. At the time, Cleveland was in last place in the region and near the bottom of all 65 Xerox offices in the nation. Frank Pacetta jumped at the opportunity.

When he arrived in Cleveland in January 1988, he found an office bereft of motivation and pride. Discipline was poor, and a sense of despair hung in the air. Frank called a meeting of all the sales representatives and their managers. "The first thing you have to do with your troops is tell them where they are going," he says. "So I told them that our goal was to make the Cleveland district number one in the region." As he looked into the eyes of the salespeople in the audience and watched their body language, he realized that achieving his goal was going to take more than an occasional motivational speech. Frank Pacetta believes the keys to success are accountability, communication, empowerment, and expectation, and with them he was able transform the sales office from its near-last place in the company to first place.

Accountability

Frank believes that everyone must be responsible for their actions, and it was this belief that helped him reshape the Cleveland office. He arrived in Cleveland and found sales reps sitting in the coffee shop at 10 A.M. The first thing he did was to lead by personal example. He was in the office every morning by 7:00 and the place was humming by 7:30. If he had to have a sales meeting, it was over by 8:30, and every single day people knew they had to be at their first appointment before 9 A.M.

Next, he needed to know what the goal for the office was going to be, and he needed to see how well they were progressing toward it. He maintains that goals should not be arbitrary numbers set by management. Instead, the reps should establish them in consultation with their sales managers, who might need to tweak the numbers a little. Pacetta holds the salesperson accountable for the numbers to which they committed. He established a review procedure with 30-, 60-, and 90-days-out columns so a rep could see what he has in the pipeline. Although that salesperson may have just had a fantastic month, if Pacetta sees there is nothing "in the bucket" for 60 to 90 days out, he is in trouble. By the time that period arrives, it will be too late to generate sales and that could cost the rep their President's Club qualification for the year. By noticing the hole well in advance, the salesperson and the sales management staff can launch an action plan to line up some prospective customers.

Communication

For Pacetta, clear communication is critically important. Wars have been fought, marriages have failed, friendships have ended, and customers have been lost because of an inability to communicate effectively. Pacetta is fastidious about communicating clearly with both his sales force and his customers. He starts each office meeting by highlighting those who have attained a significant achievement. "Praise does not cost you a dime," he says, "yet it is so good for everyone to hear." He says he wants sales reps and managers to know that the numbers they give him each year are not just grandiose figures that are meant to look good. He considers them commitments to him and to the company. In Cleveland, product knowledge was one area in which the sales staff was communicating poorly. "I not only expect my salespeople to be able to recite the features and benefits of our products in their sleep," says Pacetta, "I also want them to know all about our competitors' products." He tells them that he wants them to know a Canon machine, for example, better than the Canon rep does. Why? Because although he will not condone their badmouthing a competitor, he expects them to be able to respond to a client on how the Xerox alternative has better benefits than the other guy's product.

Pacetta emphasizes the need for product familiarity by periodically springing pop quizzes on the sales force to test their knowledge of both Xerox equipment and that of competing companies. To make it fun, Frank awards prizes to those with the best results. "In this business, what you do not know can hurt you," he says.

Upon arriving in Cleveland, his first priority, which he began on day one, was to talk to existing customers to find out what Xerox was doing right and wrong. It was a sobering experience, yet it is a practice he continues to this day. In fact, he goes one step further and invites corporate executives from Xerox headquarters in Rochester, New York—people who rarely, if ever, see a client—to go out with his sales team and listen to customer reactions. "Customer satisfaction is one of our primary objectives now-adays," he says. "Frankly, it was not always that way. When quality and service went down, so did our market share. In 1975, Xerox had 80 percent of the office copier market. By 1982, just seven years later, that had dropped to 13 percent. Today, we shoot for 100 percent total customer satisfaction. Ninety-eight percent is just not good enough. When our salespeople visit customers, they know they need to listen and respond immediately to any dissatisfaction. Taking care of a minor annoyance today prevents a major complaint later."

Empowerment

This superstar sales manager has turned the traditional authority pyramid upside down. One way he does this, as was mentioned earlier, is by having his sales agents set their own production goals. He also allows them to quote the terms they need to close a sale. Once Frank Pacetta has had a chance to see that a sales rep is reliable and worthy of trust, he empowers them to make decisions that, historically, needed management approval. "Our people run their territory as if it were their own small business. They know what they have to do to be successful, and it rarely revolves solely around price. If it did, we would not need highly trained salespeople; we could get by with a bunch of order takers." Pacetta teaches his salespeople to show the customer the difference between initial price and total value. That very point was the key to winning an order where they replaced 82 Toshiba copiers with Xerox machines. By first communicating the company's needs and objectives to the sales force and then giving them some of the toughest, most highly regarded training in any industry, Frank feels confident empowering them to do whatever it takes to bring in the orders.

Expectation

With Frank Pacetta, a clear understanding of what is expected, from all parties, is necessary. At his very first meeting with the Cleveland staff, Pacetta set the ground rules for how his sales office would be run. The sales representatives learned exactly what they could expect from him and what he expected from them.

Gaining a clear understanding of what the customer expects can be more difficult, however, because they can have differing, sometimes conflicting, expectations. One member of the customer's staff may have unreasonable expectations that they conceived unilaterally. Others may grasp at a statement made by the salesperson during the presentation and take it as a promise. One way to reduce such potential conflicts, according to Pacetta, is to always use detailed written proposals that clearly illustrate the supplier's commitments.

Phenomenal Results from Team Cleveland

By the end of Pacetta's first year in Cleveland, the sales office had been transformed. His sales staff had become a close-knit, motivated team. Enthusiasm and pride for their office were at an all-time high. In 1988, they finished first in the region and number four nationwide. The next year was even better. Ditto for 1990. In 1991, while the country was mired in one of the deepest recessions in decades, the Cleveland office broke $104 million in sales—an 85 percent increase since he had walked into the office four years earlier.

"*I* did not do it. They did it," he says today, referring to his sales reps and sales managers. He notes that for some of them it has been a difficult road.

> This is no longer Xerox, the-only-show-in-town-which-makes-copiers-company. We call ourselves "Xerox, the document company" because today we cover multiple applications. One of the barriers that prevent salespeople from moving to the next level is that they become stuck doing things the way they have always done them. In the old days,

we would cold-call and ask for the purchasing agent. Copier sales reps have used that same contact forever, but that proves they do not understand today's customers or our present solutions.

Nowadays, long before we ever suggest a product, we ask questions of many different people in the customer's organization. What are their four or five key documents? Where are their document processing bottlenecks? We want to talk with upper management, the computer department, marketing, the shipping department, the director of training. How are their sales manuals put together? Which mainframe are they using? We gear our entire compensation plan at Xerox to selling a cross section of our products. The sales rep who still thinks about just selling copy machines is going to have a very difficult time.

On a Familiar Road Again

In 1992, Frank was promoted again, this time to district manager in Columbus, Ohio, and he moved back to his wife's hometown and to the office where he had started his career. He inherited an office that was 50th out of the company's 67 districts nationwide. In one year he led the mid-Ohio district to the number one profit spot in the country, proving that his accomplishment in Cleveland was not a fluke.

It is evident that Frank Pacetta hires good people. He says that is the first important ingredient to a successful sales team. When his sales managers interview, they use a consensus approach. Each of the eight sales managers interviews the candidate separately. They are not as interested in finding out about their grade point average as they are in discovering their values. The managers must be unanimous in their recommendation of that individual. Why? Because nine months later when he is going through a tough spell, Frank does not want to hear one of them say "See, I told you I did not think much of that guy."

The benchmark is, will this person be as good as his best sales rep? Once the sales managers have all agreed that the person would be a great addition to the team, Frank interviews them. It is not the traditional interview, either. "I might ask 'Who is your role model, and why?' or 'Pretend I am your customer. Now sell me this desk.' If they go into a panic attack then, how can I believe they will not fall apart when a real customer gives them a couple of hard objections? I want to find out what is under their facade. I am also looking for people with whom my team and our customers will have fun working. You cannot be too quick to hire. If you take the time to hire the right people, your turnover rate will go way down." His father taught him the same thing by using the saying that you can beat a donkey all day long and it will still just stand there. Yet give a thoroughbred a gentle tap and it will run all day.

Frank Pacetta says the average salesperson at Xerox earns around $70,000 annually, with good people exceeding $100,000 when they have a big year. He says that thanks to the company's rigorous selection and training criteria, he has seen some outstanding professionals on various Xerox sales teams.

Admiring the Selling Skills of Others

"The best salesman I ever knew was my best friend, Steve Urban," he says. "He was so pure, so trustworthy and sincere. His customers loved him. I have been with him and have seen customers light up when he walked into their office. His follow-up was impeccable, and he could make a copy machine sound like two weeks in Maui." Pacetta explains, sadly, that his friend was killed in a traffic accident several years ago.

Frank says he loves the art of selling and enjoys seeing it done well even when it has nothing to do with Xerox, as the following incident shows.

I buy my clothes from a salesman called Doad Edwards here in Columbus. I know I could pay less elsewhere, but I just hate trying on clothes. Doad knows my size, my style, and my color preferences. I will call him up, and when I stop by an hour or so later he has everything picked out, exactly what I am looking for, complete with matching accessories.

I recently had to attend a management meeting out of town. I called Doad a few days beforehand and told him I wanted to take a new suit with me. As usual, when I stopped by, everything was waiting, but as I was packing on Sunday afternoon, my wife, Julie, suggested that I try the suit on. To my surprise, the pants legs were much too long. I called Doad at the store and told him I would simply take one of my other suits, but he would not hear of it. He came to my house, picked up the new pants and took them to his tailor. Then a couple of hours later—on a Sunday evening—he returned the correctly adjusted clothes to my home. Now I ask you, am I ever going to buy a suit from someone else in Columbus?

Recovering from Lost Opportunities

Frank Pacetta has worked at Xerox for close to 20 years, and there are probably customers today who can tell similar stories using Pacetta as the example. Unlike his efforts to resuscitate the Cleveland and Columbus district sales, however, not every presentation has led to a successful conclusion. He had a situation in Cleveland where his team was bidding for 300 machines. He felt they had done the best job and was sure they would get the business. At the end of the day, however, he was shocked to find out that they had lost it. "When I analyzed the case," he recalls, "I realized that we had not been flexible enough, that I had not played enough of a devil's advocate with the sales rep, and in a word, that we had underestimated the competition. A 300-machine order sure would have helped our sales target, and I was very angry with myself for letting the sale slip away. Nevertheless, I learned from the loss and we have never repeated that scenario."

Salespeople recently sought his advice in another tricky sales situation. There was an individual in the purchase-making position within a prospective customer's organization who simply disliked Xerox no matter what they presented. For two years Frank's sales representative had been doggedly pursuing this opportunity. He had discovered that the Xerox equipment was a perfect solution to their needs. It would have made a positive impact on the customer's productivity and bottom line, yet the Xerox salesperson was turned down without a reason. He and his sales manager had done everything they had been asked to do, and the end users all agreed that the Xerox solution was ideal. Yet the order, worth $2 million immediately in addition to a substantial value in future purchases, was turned down point-blank by this one person.

Pacetta considered his options, then decided to go over the grudge-bearer's head. "I know I took a huge risk, but I saw no alternative," he says. "Besides, if I am not taking risks, I am not doing anything to take me to a higher level. The result was that those at the top accepted the wisdom of our proposal and the earlier refusal was overruled. We made the sale."

Fighting for the Customer

Although he went over the buyer's head on that occasion, he has also taken the buyer's side in fighting Xerox's policies on behalf of the customer. "We had a small office supply company in Cleveland that had ambitious expansion plans and wanted the special terms that are reserved for Xerox's largest accounts," he says. "Although they had only one location, I fought for their request with the senior credit people at our headquarters. I finally won, and the customer did make good on their expansion plans. They called that little company OfficeMax, and today there are Xerox copiers in every one of their 375 stores around the country. It's true, I do fight for my customers, because if I don't, who will?"

Getting Personal about Competition

Fighting, figuratively speaking, is something Frank Pacetta takes seriously. He will fight for his customers and for a staff member who he believes has been treated unfairly. Every day he declares war on his competition, and "No retreat, no surrender!" was his battle cry to rally the troops against the onslaught of competitors in Cleveland. Pacetta believes that with some salespeople, you have to personalize competition to make the seriousness sink in. When he first became a sales manager, he would call his salespeople around and tell each of them to get out their wallets and look inside. He would tell them that when they let their competitor get to the appointment first, or when they could not show that the benefits of the Xerox model were greater than what the competitors could offer, they were letting the competition take money right out of their wallets.

"I used to tell my sales team in Columbus to paste photographs of their major rivals on their bathroom mirror," Pacetta recalls. "As they prepared for work each morning, they would glare at the picture and say, 'You have had it today, buddy. I'm gonna clean your clock.'" Some might consider that a little extreme, but others would agree that it puts the salesperson in the right frame of mind to start his or her day. It is the mark of a leader rather than of just a manager. "There is a difference between the two," says Pacetta. "Most businesses today are over-managed and under-led."

Listen to Frank for a while and you realize that many of the highlights of his life revolve around his times at Xerox Corporation, the only company for which he has ever worked. His eyes dance as he talks about the celebrations the Cleveland sales team had when he took them on a road trip for exceeding his wildly optimistic goals. His razor-sharp mind reels off names, dates, and details of victories along his pathway to sales success. He glows with pride as he tells stories of sales representatives who were on the point of failing when he adopted them; how they gained inspiration, direction, and hope and became highly successful salespeople or sales managers.

Frank Pacetta's Top Ten List for Sales Excellence

Frank Pacetta was profiled in a front-page article in *The Wall Street Journal* in 1991 in which the reporter described the "maverick manager's" success in Cleveland. Frank showed his Top Ten Tips to the *Journal* and they printed them with his story. They have since been copied and pinned to bulletin boards around the country:

1. Prepare customer proposals on evenings and weekends.
2. Never say "No" to a customer.
3. Make customers feel good about you, not just your product.
4. Meet customer requirements, even if it means fighting your own bureaucracy.
5. Do things for your customer you don't get paid for.
6. Know your competitor's product better than your competitor does.
7. Be early for meetings.
8. Dress and groom yourself sharply so you look like a superior product.
9. When it's time to go home, make one more telephone call.
10. If you stay in the shower a long time in the morning because you don't look forward to work, find yourself another job.

In 1994, Pacetta co-authored *Don't Fire Them, Fire Them Up: A Maverick's Guide to Motivating Yourself and*

Your Team with Roger Gittines. Some of his proudest achievements are his standings at the top of both the customer satisfaction charts and the employee contentment ratings nationwide. "They result in the same thing," he suggests. "The best way to have customer satisfaction is to have employee satisfaction. Keeping the customer happy is paramount, but it is really quite easy. You are open and honest, you meet their needs, and when you recommend a product which they subsequently buy, you do not love 'em and leave 'em. If they bring something to your attention, even if it is a minor complaint or something that is not your direct responsibility, you say, 'I will handle it for you,' and then get it done—immediately!"

Frank Pacetta is a sales manager for our times. He has earned the right to occupy his management position through his outstanding performance of every task to which he was assigned. Not only has he taken entire office territories from last place to first, he has also taken salespeople who were close to their termination point and inspired them to be truly great producers. His management tactics blend the traditional ingredients of hard work, competitive knowledge, and superior products with modern philosophies and skills such as empowerment, effective communication, and total customer satisfaction.

So where does a sales superstar go from here, when he has accumulated all these credits by his early forties? "Goals change as you progress in your career," he says. "As I mentioned, when I first joined Xerox, my goal was figuring out what I was going to do with the next paycheck. Then as I got serious about my career, I thought, 'I would like to run my own district one day.' And here I am. Three or four years ago I thought, 'I am going to run this company one day.' But things change, values change in importance. I have a wife who is delighted here in her hometown, and two kids who are very happy and active in school. I want to be able to be there at their sports practices and ballet recitals, just like my dad always was for me. I am no less ambitious than he was. I love trying to win. I might not end up with the big title, but what has been really important to me, professionally, is that I really like saying I'm from Xerox. I am still proud of the way that sounds. That has never changed, and I hope it never will."

Danielle Shepherd

★

Rosenbluth's High-Flying Superstar

For as long as corporations have needed to send their staff on business trips they have forged relationships with travel agencies. For most of this century, travel arrangements have been supplied by the corner mom and pop business, or perhaps by the agency with whom a senior officer has a relationship. In the last decade, however, everything has changed as "mega-agencies" have come to dominate the business travel scene.

Three companies overshadow all others: American Express, which in 1994 further strengthened its position as the largest agency by acquiring industry giant Thomas Cook; Carlson Wagons-Lits; and Philadelphia-based Rosenbluth International. The company began as Rosenbluth Travel, and it was founded in 1892 by Marcus Rosenbluth as a channel for East European immigrants who wanted to pay their relatives' passage to this country from their ethnic homelands. For the next 80 years, although the business grew to be the largest retail travel agency in the Philadelphia area, it remained very much a regional firm. When Hal Rosenbluth, the present CEO and great-grandson of Marcus, took over in 1985, things began to change quickly. He set his sights on growth in the corporate travel sector and aggressively pursued opportunities in that market. Rosenbluth saw its revenue grow 7,500 percent in 15 years—

from $20 million to $1.6 billion—while maintaining profits above the industry average.

"We have 23 sales associates [at Rosenbluth, all 3,000 employees are 'associates'] who are at the leading edge of our commercial sales campaign," says Vicki Looney, vice president of sales. "Our competition has deep pockets and guns for us in a very big way, yet we continue to gain market share. A salesperson for one of our competitors is considered exceptional if they generate $3–$5 million a year. Our people do double and triple that." When the author asked that the company nominate a candidate for this book, their response was immediate and unanimous: Danielle Shepherd.

One's first impression of Danielle Shepherd is that she does not seem like a salesperson. Her refined dress, gentle voice, and empathetic manner suggest perhaps a minister's wife. Then as she opens up, one sees the reason for her success in the selling profession. Her enthusiasm and company pride show through. Her attitude is always positive and her non-threatening approach conveys the impression that her goal really is to solve problems, not to make a sale.

An Unlikely Career

Sales was the vocation farthest from Shepherd's mind for most of her life. She attended Georgetown University, graduating with a degree in Russian. Long before it became her job, travel was in her blood. In 1970, she was part of the first semester-long study program for U.S. students at Leningrad University in the USSR. Several subsequent trips honed her language skills, and after graduation she ran the summer exchange program for an international student organization. Shepherd was also called on to assist in managing several cultural trips and business, environmental, and economic missions.

She moved to the Philadelphia area when she married her husband, a professor of Russian at Bryn Mawr College. Danielle subsequently held several positions with the International Visitor's Council and the International Business Forum, ultimately serving as their executive director. "It gave me a wonderful opportunity to get to know the city," she says. "I was exposed to sales for the first time, since an important part of my duties was to sell senior executives on joining the organization." When her daughter was born, however, she elected to resign so that she could devote all her time to the new responsibilities at home. "While I enjoyed being with my daughter, it was not an easy adjustment for me to stay at home," she says of her four-year hiatus.

In 1987, she heard that Rosenbluth was looking for a salesperson and applied for the position. Although she did not have a background in sales, Danielle believed that her experience in other areas would help her get the job. She felt her lack of previous selling experience would be outweighed by her interpersonal and intercultural background. Working with groups of international visitors on cultural exchanges and official visits had given her confidence in speaking to corporate gatherings. She also hoped that her track record of interacting with executives, both individually and in group presentations, would interest them. "I started right from scratch in the travel industry," she explains. "My first task was to learn the business very well. I felt I was quite familiar with the international side, and the company was thorough in training me in the areas with which I was unfamiliar."

Initially she was responsible for soliciting corporate travel accounts within the metropolitan Philadelphia area. At first her ambition was just to be successful at her job. She admits that she is not the type of person to make a 10-year life plan, but as time went on she grew to like the field of travel sales and, especially, her company. She reset her sights a little higher, deciding she would like to do well enough to move up into management. Money alone was not what motivated Danielle. "Remuneration is nice," she says, "but making a difference to people is what motivates me. Rosenbluth is an interesting company, and it has grown astronomically since I joined the firm."

Shepherd started with Rosenbluth in May 1987 and made her first sale on July 1st. "I still remember it well," she says. "It was a law firm which we would classify as a medium-sized account. I was in competition with several other agencies and had to give a final presentation to their selection committee. Since it was my first one, I was quite nervous. The normal procedure is for the committee to hear each agency's presentation and then decide among themselves who is the winner. As I finished my presentation they said, 'I think we're going to give you the business.' It was so unusual for that to happen, it sure felt great. I remember coming back to the office and excitedly telling our vice president the news.

From that moment, Danielle Shepherd's sales career has been on a fast track. Rosenbluth's approach to commercial accounts is different from that used by most of its competitors. At Rosenbluth, the salesperson is the account's primary contact through the solicitation phase. Frequently that involves fact-finding interviews, pricing negotiations, and full-scale presentations to a selection committee that will often include at least one corporate officer. When the customer awards their business to Rosenbluth, a team leader and staff of reservations agents are dedicated to that account and the team leader handles future customer service responsibilities. Unlike in other companies, where the salesperson is responsible for not only getting but also servicing the account, the Rosenbluth salesperson's primary concern is opening the account. Once that is accomplished, they go on to do the same thing with the next prospect.

Be Prepared: A Sales Professional's Motto

The process of bidding for an account can last six months and is frequently very stressful, something that Danielle seems to deal with easily. She tells of one recent case where she had been meeting with a vice president during the fact-gathering stage. The executive was well organized and very intelligent, and Danielle felt she had developed a very good rapport with him. Before her presentation to the selection committee, she had gone over the proposal with him and had discussed the agenda. They agreed in advance on the areas to be covered, and Danielle showed up for the meeting with presentation packets for the top brass, which included the company president.

After they had exchanged initial niceties, the vice president pulled out her proposal and told her that he had changed his mind, that they would not need the presentation packets. She recalls that instead, he wanted her to discuss certain points in the proposal in detail.

> For two hours without a break he machine-gunned question after question at me. When he was not asking questions, the others were. I crawled out of there totally exhausted, but I got the account! I try to analyze my presentations to learn how to make the next one better, and as I thought about this one, it dawned on me that the vice president wanted to impress his president. That is why he bombarded me with two hours of questions. It taught me to always be completely familiar with each aspect of my presentation, that I had to be able to defend every single point, anytime. I also learned never to put myself in a situation of three against one again. If I discover there will be three or four client representatives present, I know to take another team member from Rosenbluth with me.

No matter how prepared a salesperson may be, there will be times when they do not know the answer to a question. If a salesperson is eager to win an account, says Shepherd, such situations may tempt them to give affirmative answers to some questions that they cannot truthfully answer. "You simply cannot do that," she warns. "It will come back to haunt you. If I do not know something or am not sure we can deliver a requested service, I will always check first, then answer the client. I never want to promise something I cannot deliver."

Maintaining Professionalism
Even When You Lose

Danielle Shepherd says that no matter how many sales successes she has enjoyed, no salesperson can expect to win every prospect. Her most disappointing loss was a company that had said "No" every time she simply asked for the opportunity to submit a proposal. After several years of Shepherd's persistence, they finally agreed to talk to her. "At first, I thought we had no chance of penetrating this account," she says. "Then the more we talked, the more they seemed to really like me. As it got close to the decision, they eliminated several other competitors and we made it to the final round." That glimmer of hope grew brighter as Shepherd heard reports of company insiders saying wonderful things about Rosenbluth.

"It really looked like they were going to select us," she sighs. "Then, at the very end, they said 'We think you are really good, but we have decided to go with another agency.' It was a political connection that made the difference. Nevertheless, it did hurt. I went from figuring it was a hopeless case, to believing we had a 90 percent chance at the account, to zero." As disappointing as the loss was, Danielle was gracious in defeat. "I maintained all my contacts there," she adds, "and assured them I was here if they ever needed us. You must show your professionalism even when you lose a customer."

In another situation where the customer had not selected Rosenbluth International, her contact at the company—a large bank—called her several months later and asked how quickly Rosenbluth could install their own travel department. Danielle was told that the other agency had mismanaged a trip for the bank president and that if Rosenbluth could be up and running in 30 days, the account was theirs. She says her initial thought was that it was a dream—or a joke. Quickly discovering that the call was for real, she sprang into action.

> We usually allow a minimum of 60–90 days to initiate service for a new customer. However, everybody in our company pulled out all the stops this time and delivered in 30 days, as promised. It has turned out to be a very nice account. The key point is that over any company's 103-year history, you are going to lose some customers. My emphasis

here is that you must always maintain positive, professional, ongoing relationships with them, because you never know when they will be looking to change agencies again. It is just like when I make cold calls, looking for new accounts. There will be more "No" than "Yes" responses. You have to just pick yourself up and throw yourself into the next opportunity. It is essential that you maintain a positive attitude, despite the personal peaks and valleys we all encounter. There are other things in life than losing an account.

Coping with Fear, Worry, and Pain

One of Danielle's valleys came in 1991, when she discovered that she had breast cancer. She never told her clients about it unless there was a reason they had to know. Despite the side effects from the chemotherapy treatments, she felt challenged to continue working. She says work kept her focused on things other than the cancer. "I had a positive attitude when I came here, but after the breast cancer, I learned more about positive attitudes than I had in my entire life," she says today. She has become very active in the issues surrounding breast cancer, and is still quite involved in a support group. There have been horror stories about women who were denied promotions—even given pink slips—after being diagnosed with the disease, and this motivates her continued volunteer commitment to the cause.

"The people here were just fantastic," she says. "Rosenbluth was incredibly supportive, from Hal himself to Vicki Looney, senior management, and my co-workers—they were at my side every moment. They sent cards to cheer me up, called with words of encouragement and reassurance, they even chased me out of the office if they thought I was spending too much time there."

The executive staff went beyond that. In the early part of 1992, as Danielle's recovery from surgery was progressing, Rosenbluth International was planning an enormous celebration for that summer to commemorate its 100th anniversary. The company enthusiastically endorsed Danielle's idea of holding a breast cancer awareness seminar run by the oncologists and nurses who treated her at Presbyterian Hospital.

For several incredible days in the summer of 1992, associates, suppliers, and invited guests were treated to "Live the Spirit V" in Philadelphia. This cornucopia of special events ranged from personal development seminars to travel industry workshops and parties. Danielle did not know if anyone would show up for an event as sobering as a cancer seminar and was astonished to have several hundred women attend the workshop. In a year filled with distractions, distress, and pain, Danielle Shepherd still opened $5 million in new accounts. Her co-workers and managers bestowed the Live the Spirit Award on her for her inspirational attitude and accomplishments.

Learning from Other Salespeople

Shepherd frequently uses the professionalism of salespeople in other fields as a guide to decide to whom she will direct her own business. "I just went out yesterday to buy a carpet for my daughter's room," she reveals. "We went first to a carpet outlet that heavily advertises its low prices. At five minutes to four, the salesperson made it clear that the store was about to close. He could not have cared less about our needs. We drove to Sears and their salesman gave wonderful service. He took pains to explain the pads, the delivery schedule, and everything he thought might be useful. I ordered the carpet on the spot and his last words were, 'Make sure you call me if the delivery is not there on time, or if you have any other questions.' You see, sales ability has nothing to do with price, but everything to do with determining a client's needs and then providing a solution to them."

Asked whom Shepherd considers the top salesperson she has ever met, she answers that Vicki Looney is the best she has seen. "She is really good," she continues. "First, she listens. That is the most important thing we need to do for a client, listen to their needs. She also articulates very well and does so in a way that matches our benefits to the needs the customer has described. I have learned far more from her than from any motivational tape series."

Balancing the Demands of Work and Home

Danielle Shepherd acknowledges that the selling profession has many demands that can conflict with one's personal life.

> It is a challenge, keeping a balance between work and my home responsibilities. Luckily, I have a lot of support within my family, but every so often, I have to sit down and ask, "Have I been spending too much time away from them because of work?" If so, I take a day off, go to the ballet with my daughter, or we do something fun as a family. I sometimes talk to salespeople at Rosenbluth or at our suppliers. Different barriers pose challenges to them, but I see it as critical for us to identify our own strengths and weaknesses and take action to improve on them. As salespeople, we sometimes let our egos get in the way, and that can be a serious mistake. We do not need to trumpet it to the world, but it is important that we admit to ourselves, "This is an area I have to work on." Then follow through and do it.

Shepherd knows that she needs to constantly hone her skills and stay at the forefront of what is going on in her industry. Another of her personal challenges is time management. Sales is a demanding profession, and she says that it sometimes seems there are not enough hours in the day both to do her part at home and to execute her sales plans. That is why she has to force herself to prioritize her tasks to maximize every minute of the day.

Looking for Leads

The Rosenbluth policy of turning ongoing account service over to a team formed for that purpose gives Danielle the time to prospect for new business. "I use several means of finding potential customers," she explains. "We choose not to buy leads. Instead I look for articles on companies that are moving to the area, or that are hiring, in such sources as the daily newspaper, business journals, and Chamber of Commerce reports. I also network with suppliers and civic organizations. Cold-calling is a part of the job. It is not particularly pleasant, but it is one of the things we have to do to reach a higher level of success, so you do it."

She explains that one frustration peculiar to her industry is the lack of standardization about which person or department coordinates all the business travel in an organization. "That person may be in human resources in one company, the chief financial officer in another, and in the purchasing department in the next firm. I call it 'Dialing for Dollars,'" she laughs, putting a positive spin on what every salesperson considers the dreariest of tasks.

Moving on Up

Danielle has been the top salesperson in the region several times and is often in the top five of the company. She has been offered promotions twice. She declined the first offer because of her desire to spend time nearer home when her daughter was younger, and the second after discovering her cancer. She has recently accepted a third offer of advancement and is now a regional sales manager. "Although I now manage two sales associates, I am still on the front line with customers every day," she says. "We do a lot of role playing, and I love playing the client. I have learned a lot by watching other salespeople try to sell me in that role. I tell the salespeople I work with that the keys to success in keeping clients happy are simple: know your product, satisfy their needs, respond quickly when they call, and above all, be honest. How difficult is that? I really enjoy seeing the salespeople succeed; it is the best reward there is. Despite all the technology and new business theories, it still comes down to our need to be the high quality/low cost supplier of travel services in the industry."

Shepherd says that to achieve that objective, one has to be totally honest with the client from the outset. If she absolutely has to reduce the price, she can do it, but Rosenbluth may have to cut back on the services they offer the account. "Instead of answering their phone in 10 seconds when they call the travel department," she explains, "it might take 20 seconds. I tell the customer, 'We do not sell widgets, we sell service, and we can slice it and dice it any way you want.' I am a relationship person. I'm not looking for the quick sale, and neither is my company. We want long-term relationships with our customers. We have to see every proposal as a win-win partnership or it is not worth my time, or anybody's time, to go after the business."

The Company's Philosophy

Hal Rosenbluth, the thirty-something great-grandson of the company's founder, set a few tongues wagging when he took over as chief executive in 1985. He was young, his ideas were radical, and he wanted to attain his goals quickly. It did not matter that the people doing the sniping were other local travel agencies who lacked the vision Hal brought to his company. What Hal Rosenbluth did, before terms like "reinventing the company" became fashionable, was to focus everything not on the customer, but on the employee.

In his book with the provocative title *The Customer Comes Second*, he writes, "All too often companies bring stress, fear, and frustration to their people—feelings they bring home to their families each night. This creates problems at home which people bring back to work in the morning." Since those people interact with customers all day long, it is logical that the unhappy employee is likely to provide a less than excellent level of service to those clients. By creating a pleasant, team-oriented workplace where the focus is on employee satisfaction, the second priority—the customer—is actually treated better.

Not long after these innovations were launched, good things started to happen at Rosenbluth. *The Wall Street Journal, Inc.* magazine, and the *Harvard Business Review* ran complimentary stories featuring the firm's success. Rosenbluth International was also placed in the top 10 in the book *The 100 Best Companies to Work for in America.* Tom Peters, considered a global guru on the topic of service excellence, says that Hal Rosenbluth's story is "one of the great, unsung business success sagas of the eighties and nineties. Put your front-line employees first if you are serious about putting your customers first."

While the accolades were coming from the outside, the company's values were winning new customers at an awesome rate. In 15 years it has grown from eight Philadelphia-area offices and a few dozen staff members to the third-largest travel agency in the world, with more than 1,000 locations in 41 countries, staffed by over 3,000 associates. Most important, when sales superstars (a politically incorrect term at team-oriented Rosenbluth) like Danielle Shepherd open new accounts in this fiercely competitive industry, the company has a client retention rate of 96 percent.

"Danielle Shepherd is a success because of what she brings to the table," suggests Vicki Looney. "She is well educated and articulate, and those are fine assets. I see many salespeople and I'll tell you, Danielle has something else. She has enthusiasm and flexibility. She interfaces well with both senior officers and entry-level employees. In an industry that is constantly changing, she is not threatened by change, she is excited by it. She is a great communicator and the epitome of a team player." Looney hesitates as if, despite the list of commendable attributes, she is missing the key adjective. Then she suddenly finds it. "Danielle has a *spark* that simply sets her apart. Any company with a Danielle Shepherd to be a success."

Bill Coble

★

The Down-Home Guy from GE

Meeting the *real* Bill Coble is quite a surprise. When his company, General Electric, nominated him as a sales superstar, they used language such as "in the top ranks of our sales force for a number of years." It led one to expect a slick, three-piece suited MBA corporate type. The real Bill Coble seems more like Mister Rogers. "Well, hi! Welcome to North Carolina. Let me take your jacket. Here, put your feet up and make yourself at home," says the affable Coble in his rich Tarheel drawl. One feels immediately at ease—probably the same way his longtime customers feel when he pulls off the dusty southern roads to see them. "Oh, good. It's Bill. Take a load off. Y'want some iced tea?"

For Bill Coble, selling has been his life, and other than a four-year stint in the air force, selling appliances has been his only vocation. Thirteen or 14 times he has won the top sales spot among the GE appliance sales force of several hundred, and he is perpetually in the top 10. Coble's sales success comes not from selling to mega-stores in New York or Chicago, but to smaller outlets in the area around his North Carolina birthplace.

"I started with Westinghouse and spent 12½ good years with them," he says. "However, they decided to get out of the appliance business, and GE, their big competitor,

199

created a position for me here in Charlotte. That was 24 years ago, and I have sold to some customers that entire time. I enjoyed it from the moment I first got into it."

A Long Love Affair with Selling

"Sales is a great business. I remember as a young man, after I'd been selling for just three months, getting a call from a regional manager in Ohio telling me that I earned more than he did. Where else can a person with one year of college enjoy job stability and great perks like trips to exotic resorts? I meet really pleasant people every day, pretty much set my own schedule, and can earn as much as I want."

In fact, Bill Coble is the only person in history to win the coveted Masters Award—the company's most prestigious sales achievement—five times. Since 1964, Bill has sold major appliances such as refrigerators, washers, dryers, ranges, and televisions to retail stores. In 1985, GE realigned their product mix, and his division lost their television lines. A substantial chunk of his revenue disappeared with the televisions.

Long before Charlotte became a boom town, Coble was recognized as a top salesman. "I received letters from the chairman of Westinghouse praising my sales accomplishments and enclosing a diamond pin just about every year I was with them," he recalls. General Electric has about 300 salespeople in the appliances division, 18 of whom are in the Carolinas. As shy as he is to talk about his own achievements, Coble does reveal that he is generally the top salesperson in the region. "Put it this way, I'm highly unhappy if I'm much lower than number two," he allows.

His Secrets to Sales Success

He attributes his sales success to hard work and taking care of the customer's problems right away. "If you take care of

their needs and concerns immediately, they will buy from you," he adds. "When someone asks you to do something, they expect you to do it almost instantly, not two weeks later." Coble recalls that values were different three-and-a-half decades ago, but sales were not necessarily any easier to make "We've always had competition, from big, well-known companies such as Whirlpool, Frigidaire, and the like, so it has never been easy. It comes down to building rapport with a dealer. Once we have established a relationship of trust and respect, the sale is easier to make."

Bill chuckles as he tells how he used to call on the elderly owner of one appliance store who never could remember his name. He always called Coble "Mr. Westinghouse." Bill never thought much of it until he joined GE. Although the dealer remembered that the salesman had switched companies, he continued to call Coble "Mr. Westinghouse." Twenty-four years after he joined General Electric, Bill has sold him rail carloads of GE appliances, yet to this day he still calls him "Mr. Westinghouse." "So long as he puts 'GE' on the purchase order, I guess I can live with it!" Bill muses.

Coble says that building trust with prospective customers is a critical early requirement. "You build trust by taking care of their problem when you said you would," he says. "Especially in today's business climate, customers do not believe they owe you anything." According to Coble, it does not matter which firm you are with, you have to earn their trust and respect first. Coble says that when you walk into a prospective customer's office, you had better believe he is thinking to himself, "I don't owe anything to you, why should I buy something from you?" He feels salespeople need to look beyond the features of their product and show the buyer how what they are selling will help him increase sales, profits, and satisfied customers. Nowadays, according to Coble, you have to start bright and early and be prepared to stay late. "People who take a lot of time away from their selling responsibilities and customers don't last very long," he warns.

Evidently, Coble does practice what he preaches. Bill Pleasants Sr., president and owner of the four Plaza Appliance stores in Charlotte, says Bill Coble has called on him since 1972. "We have had a long business relationship that extended into a personal friendship. He has done an excellent job of helping our company grow." Pleasants says that Coble is the kind of salesperson who doesn't just come in to sell you something, that he can sense a need—even when the dealer doesn't realize he has one. He goes beyond what other salespeople do. He knows that for him to sell a dealer a truckload of appliances, the dealer has to be able to sell them quickly and profitably, one at a time. "Bill is the kind of guy who will help me develop a strategy to do that. He is a valuable salesperson for GE. They should only be so fortunate as to have more like him."

Bill Coble is a genial, laid-back kind of person. He comes across as very non-aggressive, but he can be pushed too far. He believes that salespeople cannot sugarcoat important issues that need dealing with. Even if your answers are not what the customer wants to hear, he says, people prefer to be treated in a forthright, open, and honest manner.

> I have had lots of difficult customers. It drives me crazy when they will not talk to me. The company once added Shelby, North Carolina, to my territory because my predecessor had made all the dealers there mad at us. I went in and did well, recruiting back every store except one. Finally, I was tired of being given the run-around by this one dealer, so I said to him, "Mister John, are you or are you not going to buy from me? If not, then I am going to cancel your dealer franchise." Two weeks later he took me aside when I went back to his store. "I have never had anybody talk to me like that before," he said. So I told him straight, that I did not mean to be rude, but I had to know where I stood. I got the order that day, and we have enjoyed an excellent relationship ever since.

Integrity and Interest in the Customer Pay Off

In 36 years of selling, Coble says he cannot ever recall losing a customer because they were mad at him or his company. "Certainly, a few went out of business, others merged, but I have never lost a customer to a competitor," he claims. Year after year, through product recalls, recessions, and the onslaught of foreign-built competitive models, Bill Coble's business continues to grow. "I sold about $14 million in 1993 and $16 million in 1994," he says. "My biggest year ever was $19 million, but that was when I could still sell TVs, which accounted for a major part of my sales."

"Bill Coble is genuinely interested in every individual in his customer's organization," says Jack Hodes, GE's retail regional manager in Charlotte. "From the president to the delivery boy, he shows them a can-do attitude and is always very positive." He says that no matter what he assigns as a stretch target for his salespeople, Bill Coble always figures out a way to achieve it. He says that there is no hill too high for Bill to climb. According to Hodes, many salespeople just walk into a customer's store and hope to pick up business, but not Bill. He always has a plan. He is always very tactful with his customers, and his qualities set him apart from the average salesperson.

Bill Coble is equally proud of his company. "We have many competitors out there, but the GE sales division has more integrity than any organization I know of. You have to have integrity to be successful in sales. Look at the best salesperson you know. Not somebody who has had a good year, but the person who has displayed consistent long-term success. I guarantee you will see a person with impeccable integrity and a strong work ethic.

Paying Your Dues

Bill Coble is asked whom he sees as a top-flight sales professional. "Zig Ziglar," he suggests. "In my opinion, I think he is one of the best. I have seen him and listened to him a fair bit. I reckon of anybody, Lee Iacocca is about the darned best hero I have got. He has to be the best salesperson, and the best motivator, I have ever seen. I draw many similarities between the car industry and the major appliance business."

Coble points out that Zig Ziglar and Lee Iacocca were also totally dedicated to their goals, something he finds missing in many salespeople today. "You cannot expect business to come to you," he advises. "Sitting in the office, waiting to be fed sales leads is no pathway to sales success." Yet he says he sees it all the time; salespeople get disheartened, and their interests change. The next thing you know, they're on the golf course a couple of times a week. Bill cautions salespeople that they cannot do that instead of doing the hard work: cold-calling, proposal writing, and face-to-face relationship building. "Time is the enemy of us all. It is the biggest barrier that prevents me from reaching the next level. Now I like to be busy—that helps me stay focused—but I do not have enough time in the day to get everything done. And I have a 35-year record of solid customer relationships to give me business. How on earth can someone 25 years old who is new to the business expect to be successful if they do not dedicate every minute of the working day to building their foundation?"

Mentoring New Salespeople

Evidently, Bill Coble empathizes with the next generation of aspiring sales stars, and he welcomes the opportunity to mentor them. What counsel does he provide the salesperson who just lost a big sale? "You talk to them," he responds. "You tell them they cannot make every sale. We sales reps have a lot of pride, and losing an order is tough for us. Still, it is not personal." He says that every order GE gets probably means an order has been lost by another salesperson. The salesperson needs to get the emotion out of the way and discover why they lost the order, then learn from that and go on to the next opportunity.

The Payback from Building Relationships

One appreciates the value of building solid relationships of mutual trust with the customer in Bill's next anecdote, "I suddenly realized yesterday that today was the end of our quarterly accounting period," he explains. "My orders thus far had not set the world on fire, but now I only had one day to change that. So I went out yesterday and spent the day with two dealers. By the end of the day, I had written $360,000 in sales to one store and more than $600,000 to the other. In one day, I wrote a million dollars in orders and saved the quarter for me. But you see, I could do that because of the trust and rapport I have spent 35 years developing with those customers."

Bill Coble tells how his boss called him in recently and asked for help in getting into two major utility companies. The objective was for the companies to feature GE appliances in their showrooms. Bill told him that he has a friend who is the director of sales and marketing for one company, and that he would be happy to make a couple of phone calls. "I made the calls, lined up appointments, and we sold both companies on becoming GE accounts. Now one of them will be my dealer, but I will not make a dime on the other, but I am delighted to have done it. Why? Because I've built a stronger relationship with my management and have helped my company win a couple of new customers. It also allowed me to pay back some of the many favors people did for me when I was getting started. Everybody wins!"

Everybody Wins! could well have been the title for this book. It certainly describes the trails left by the superstar salespeople after they have made the sale. Bill Coble has devoted a lifetime to establishing relationships with his customers, and those ties have endured for three decades. He built a foundation of trust at an early stage and never gave his customers reason to regret dealing with his company. His admonition to work hard and to not sit in the office waiting for leads is as sound advice today as it was in the dawning of his career. Yet once again, this salesman states that the biggest secret to his success is taking care of the customer's problems right away. Why should that be such a secret? Why is it so unusual? While his competitors try to figure that out, Bill Coble can be found at one of his dealers on the back roads of North Carolina. He wants to be there as another truckload of appliances he has sold is delivered.

"I guess I have been lucky," he says. "I have always had great customers to call on and good products to sell. Mind you, I've worked my buns off over the years. But selling has been—and still is—a whole lot of fun. I would not trade my experiences as a salesman for anything in the world."

Chris Meunier

★

Warner Lambert's Superstar in New England

Christine Meunier was a born salesperson—literally. As the only girl in a family of five brothers, all of whom chose careers in sales, perhaps they predestined her future. "I grew up in a very competitive environment," she chuckles. "I had five brothers with huge egos, and became very active in sports and learned the importance of competing to win at an early age." Today, as one of the youngest, most recognized and promoted salespeople in Warner Lambert, her brothers must surely acknowledge her as the leader of the pack.

Choosing a Career

Chris looked at several career opportunities. Her father was vice president of an insurance and financial services company, so she considered insurance along with the manufacturing and health care fields. She describes herself as a very loyal person, so it was very important for her to find an employer who would reward her contributions with long-term growth. She says that from the start she felt Warner Lambert was a great company on which to build a future, although she admits that at first she was more excited about the selling opportunities than the management potential.

209

"Coming out of college in 1985, there was no question in my mind that I wanted to go into sales," she says. "I get a lot of satisfaction from seeing the concrete results of my work." Initially the company sent her into the field as a territory rep, where she was responsible for detailing the company's product merchandise displays in retail stores. Warner Lambert produces numerous consumer health and personal care products with such recognizable brand names as Benadryl, Listerine, Lubriderm, Efferdent, and Sinutab.

Meunier has always liked working with other people to see how they sell. She says she still picks up tips today, just as she did 10 years ago, on how to better deal with certain situations. "It gives me a real thrill to see someone handle a problem in a way I have not considered before," she adds. The early days of her career were not easy for Chris. She had minimal training and experience, and she recalls that she constantly heard "No" and was barraged with objections. She even had a store manager tell her he did not want her merchandise on his shelves. She says that the technical aspect of her job was not very hard, but it was often mentally challenging. She dealt with it by leaving yesterday's rejections behind her. "I got up every morning and said, 'Today is a new day,' and it really worked. I carried the little victories with me and remembered them when I walked into the next customer's store."

Meunier recalls that she had some great trainers and mentors whom she could count on for help.

The best I have ever seen is Mark Wilson. He was my regional manager and I worked for him for two years. What a great learning experience that was. He quickly saw the things that I already knew and pinpointed my areas of weakness, helping me improve on those skills. Mark taught me that there was a lot more to know than what was in the training manuals. He would coach me after every customer call, often suggesting another approach to convey our point or showing me a new way to put a program together. He made me realize that I should never stop trying to take my knowledge and skills to the next level.

Moving up the Ladder

Chris Meunier rapidly progressed to that level in her career. Just two years after joining Warner Lambert, she was promoted to district manager. In that position she was responsible for several large key accounts and six salespeople in a territory that stretched from Maine to Connecticut. "It was one of my most rewarding jobs," she concludes today. "Not only did it give me experience managing people, it provided the opportunity to work with important accounts. I got to understand their motivation and special needs." That, in turn, helped her do a better job for the customer. Warner Lambert subsequently split those responsibilities, designating Chris as a key accounts manager and then as key customer development manager.

The company consolidated both the consumer health and personal care divisions into one selling unit, and she ended up with a vastly greater product and brand portfolio. "As I moved to that next level, I had to develop a much higher technical ability and my job was more activity based. I was responsible for the profit and loss on those key accounts." In the midst of this, the company plucked Meunier from her position and gave her a special assignment as marketing development manager.

"I learned so much during that time," she says today. "Until then, my entire focus had been on getting our products into the stores. In my new position I helped design specific marketing programs for the accounts. Instead of thinking, as I had for years, 'I have to get my sales volume up,' my concern was, 'Watch the company's bottom line with this pricing program.'" Her expanded territory included the metropolitan New York area, upstate New York, Connecticut, and New England. As the special assignment ended, Warner Lambert promoted Chris to regional director, bringing her in a full circle back to a position where she managed both key customer accounts and other salespeople.

"I have 40 people in my region," she says, "along with the responsibility of bringing profits—not just sales revenue—to the company for 30 brands and 200 SKUs (stock-keeping units). The largest account for our entire company, which I managed for six years and with which I developed some great relationships, is again my responsibility." Chris Meunier has sold her way into the express lane of the success superhighway at Warner Lambert in less than 10 years, but her goals remain relatively unchanged from those first days on the job. "I decided very early in my association with this company that I was here to stay. I would like to become a vice president one day, then work my way up to president and eventually sit on the board of directors." She recalls how she used to envision that moment, taking her seat at a board meeting, and now, years later, she still has the same vision. "I guess that means it is a good, durable goal to keep," she concludes.

Her greatest challenge as a manager comes not from her subordinates but from managing her time and administrative work, a problem she says confronts all salespeople today. She sighs as she describes how modern technology—E-mail, fax machines, and beepers—creates a barrage of paperwork that demands her immediate response. Luckily, the traits Chris learned by being a member of a large family living in a small house now come in handy. She has never needed a formal time management course. "As a kid I learned organization," she recalls. "The laundry had to go here, white socks in this drawer, the blue ones in this one." Those lessons instilled the instincts that help her prioritize and organize her management duties today.

Her Biggest Sale

Chris clearly remembers the largest sale she ever made. Warner Lambert's biggest account, a large drugstore chain, identified a need and she believed she had the right product to fill that need. Right about then two calamitous events occurred. First, her customer's store traffic took a nose dive. Second, there was a major consumer shift from buying this product in drug stores to purchasing it in other retail outlets such as mass merchandisers and supermarkets. Her big customer said they needed to buy the product at a steeply discounted price to attract customers back to their stores. "I fought them all the way, saying a cut price alone would not create loyalty or the image needed to make customers think of their company in the future," explains Meunier. "I told them the customer would not remember their store because of the one product of ours they had purchased there." She told the store's management that they needed to create the impression of added value for their customer. She then gave them the opportunity to promote another product, which Warner Lambert wanted in customers' hands, by bundling it with the original item. "They bought so much product that I was actually scared," she admits. "I dreaded how they would remember my name, both at their offices and at my own headquarters, if this promotion failed. I talked them into a great multimedia advertising campaign, using print, radio, and in-store merchandising, and guess what! They sold so much of the product they had to come back to us and buy more." Warner Lambert made a huge sale and introduced customers to their new product. The stores gained droves of new customers, and the end user got a great bargain. That was a win-win-win deal, and it did nothing to hurt Chris Meunier's sales career either.

As she reviews that successful sale with the benefit of hindsight, Chris recognizes the points that contributed to its favorable outcome and how close the situation was to becoming her biggest *lost* sale. "We had to really hang in there," she says. "It went far beyond just giving the account our product at a good discount. I would leave them one day thinking 'This is great, they are going to go for it,' then the next day I would get a call saying we were back to square one." There was much negativity to overcome, but she says the hardest part was convincing them to buy into the value-added idea. "There was some risk there for both of us, she admits. "Ultimately, perseverance and sensitivity to the customer's needs and concerns paid off."

Her Biggest Lost Sale . . . Almost

Mismanagement of that same account, Warner Lambert's biggest customer, was also Meunier's most troubling problem in her selling career. While she was on special assignment as marketing development manager, the account was given to another salesperson to service. When Chris returned to the drugstore chain, she discovered that her colleague had unloaded huge quantities of merchandise on the account. "Where they would normally maintain a 6-week supply in inventory, I found a 34-week stockpile," she says, rolling her eyes. "So much for a big 'Welcome Back!' The account said, 'You people sold it and shipped it to us. Now you must take it back.'" Not only would issuing a credit for so much stock have ruined her sales figures, but it could not have come at a worse time. Warner Lambert had just decided to downsize their marketing efforts and stock levels of that item, so there was no way her company was going to restock all that merchandise. Chris Meunier found herself in the middle of what could have potentially been a career damaging situation. On one side she had the customer telling her to either take back all of the product, or pay them $25,000 to subsidize their inventory costs, something she knew didn't have a prayer of getting approved. On the other side, Warner Lambert just wanted her to take care of the problem. "Talk about a no-win situation," she says. "I really did think that our biggest account would never buy from me again." It took many, many weeks of negotiations, but finally the customer agreed to a settlement credit that cost Warner Lambert 200 percent less than their initial demand. With that offset allowance, the customer ran a "Buy one, get one free" promotion that brought customers into their stores. Chris got her company's product in the consumer's hands without affecting their stocking objectives, the account made a little money, and everyone was happy.

"As with most worthwhile victories, this one was a long road, and at times it was scary," she adds. "I felt so good afterwards, knowing that I had helped resolve a very big problem to the benefit of all parties. In a way, that describes the whole concept of selling, doesn't it? One other nice bonus was that after we had worked it all out, I think the account had a much higher opinion of me and my company."

What Sales Reps Need

Meunier's philosophy on sales extends far beyond consumer preferences and product knowledge. She shrugs in an "aw, shucks" kind of way, and at first says—sheepishly—that she doesn't really have a formal sales philosophy. Then she goes on to stress that she simply asks herself how she would act if she were that prospect or customer. "How would we do things? How would Warner Lambert's products benefit us?" she muses, adding that by addressing the mutual risks both parties face, it is easier for her to present the benefits to the client. It also clearly puts Meunier in the mind-set that anything she is proposing has to be mutually beneficial. She sees herself as a partner with her customer, a position that helps cement long-term relationships with her buyers. "Geez, I don't know if you'd call that a selling philosophy," she says. "It's just the way I operate."

Chris says she often sees other salespeople calling on her accounts and is amazed at their lack of preparation before their visit. It is hardly surprising that some have maintained the same stagnant career level for decades. Worse yet, their companies send a new salesperson through the customer's door every few months. Many salespeople depend on their company to feed them everything they need to present to a customer. "If you picked a career in sales, you should realize it is a two-way street," she says. "Before you walk in the customer's door, you must know what you need to make that sale happen. That is your responsibility. One phone call doesn't do it, either." Meunier says that to be successful today, the salesperson had better learn everything they can about brand facts, purchasing dynamics, competing brands, customer buying preferences, and consumer shopping statistics. She is amazed that so few salespeople take time to do their homework in these areas. She believes that any salesperson who does will be set apart from most of their competitors. Meunier reveals that she still practices what she is going to say to her customer, often aloud in her car, as she drives between calls. After visiting an account, she spends several minutes quietly reviewing what happened, noting how to capitalize on those things that went well in the future.

Recognizing the Best of the Best

Warner Lambert has roughly 500 salespeople in its North American sales force, and there are two achievements that recognize the elite among the sales team. The top five salespeople in the country are selected each year for membership in the Achievers Club. Chris has won admission to it twice. The pinnacle of success, awarded to only one person each year, is the President's Club. To be considered, a salesperson must consistently generate significant overall volume, and, more importantly, must show significant increases in market share across all brand and product categories. "It is one of the most competitive challenges I have ever seen," says the woman whose five brothers taught her about competitiveness before she could talk. "It encompasses all the functions of your job. If you just do your job, you will never win." Chris Meunier was voted the President's Club winner in 1991. "I've got to tell you, it was one of the most rewarding moments I have ever experienced," she says. "It came after a very difficult year for us. I had really worked hard, all the time, and that recognition was a way of seeing that all my work had paid off. I cannot even describe what it felt like to hear them make that announcement, to go up to the podium and receive the award. There was a really nice trip afterwards, which made it even more memorable."

Chris says that having some great bosses inspired her to go beyond the expected norms in her everyday work. She remembers that in high school, when she had a teacher whom she really liked, she would study harder and put much extra effort into her work. She says that it was her way of saying thanks for helping her learn and making the experience more pleasant. "I felt the same way here. Part of that award was my way of saying thanks to the managers who have made my job in sales more pleasant and successful. I am very proud of what we do here."

Today, Chris says her greatest motivation comes from striving to be the best. She reveals that everyone in her family still takes competition very seriously, a characteristic that clearly molded her personality from childhood. She recalls all the sports she played: hockey, basketball, softball, and others. "I had to learn to hit the ball harder, to run faster, even to get better grades at school, if I was to beat my five brothers," she says. Nobody ever handed her a victory, and she expects to compete hard to win today, too.

One of her greatest challenges came in 1991 when her mother passed away. As the only daughter, Chris had always been very close to her mom. "She was the source of much of my determination. It was she who taught me I could do anything, be anything, I wanted in life. I always turned to her when I was down or depressed and she would pump me back up again." Chris admits that after her mother's death she buried herself in her work for several months. She has since learned to be far more dependent on motivating herself out of the ruts that come with any sales career. Her advice to others is simple: If you make a mistake, lose an account, or get behind in your goals, just learn from the experience and move on.

When Chris Meunier started this interview, she told of the times when she was a young girl who joined her brothers in highly competitive sporting events. As she got better, she would occasionally be the one to hit the home run or score the touchdown. She describes the exhilaration and pride she felt, saying, "I wanted to say to my brothers, 'Hey! You know what? I scored!'" Barely 10 years out of college, Chris Meunier has shown skill, agility, and staying power as she has rapidly progressed up the corporate ladder. Today, she is truly a sales superstar. Her brothers, her parents, and her colleagues at Team Warner Lambert are the ones who are now cheering, "Hey! You know what? Chris just scored again!" And the game has only just begun.

Tony Palett

★

Ameritech's Cellular Success in Motown

Quickly! Who is Ameritech's top salesperson in the automotive cellular division? Tony Palett. Who is the top salesperson in the rapidly growing factory-installed car phone industry among Ford auto dealers? Tony Palett!

It is appropriate that Palett started his career selling eye care products to ophthalmologists and optical stores, because he is a man with vision. In 1984, the very dawn of the cellular communications age, he saw the potential for this equipment that would save salespeople from having to pull off the road every time they needed to make a telephone call. "I have an ability to see what's going to sell," he says. "And I *knew* that this was going to be a big, big business. I always test myself as the potential consumer by asking, 'Is there a need for this product? Would I use it?'"

One item that he correctly perceived would sell very well was a car telephone built into the visor of the vehicle. Tony designed and built one himself. He had it patented, and his invention was subsequently installed in cars across America. His creativity has led him to develop products on which he has obtained 17 U.S. and foreign patents, all of them in the cellular communications field. When a friend from Chrysler Corporation advised him that Ameritech was looking for a salesperson for their cellular phone division in Detroit, he jumped to attention.

The Perfect Sales Career

The "Baby Bell" firm has become a telecommunications giant in the Midwest, and Palett believes he could not have written a better job description for himself. "It was a beautiful position in a brand new program," he says. "I was so happy when they picked me." His job entailed calling on Ford and Chrysler dealers and encouraging them to sell Ameritech cellular service when they sold their own telephone equipment to each car and truck customer. Despite his enthusiasm for the future of the industry, the early days in his new career were not easy.

"The products from the manufacturers were overpriced back then," he recalls. "And the auto industry salespeople were only interested in moving metal across the curbs, to use their colloquialism. Car dealers could make a great deal of money when they sold a car. They were not interested in the few extra dollars they could make by selling a car phone." Palett handled the objections by sidestepping the actual profit per unit and explained the tremendous growth the industry was experiencing. He told them that their customers would soon buy a car phone from somebody, so by delivering it to them with their new vehicle, the dealer would establish a reputation as a one-stop shop. He was successful, and more and more of the dealers he called on started recommending the equipment to their new and used car buyers.

"As technology developed, the cost of the hardware from manufacturers dropped, and with that, the dealers saw better margins," he says. "Then Ameritech added General Motors dealers to my territory. My goal was to sell the biggest Cadillac dealer in the United States—Don Massey Cadillac. Mr. Massey ordered some GM phones and told his salespeople to sell them." But the results were very disappointing to Tony Palett. "They were only interested in selling cars, not telephones," he admits. "Then one day, I came across the parts manager at Don Massey Cadillac. At this, and most dealerships nowadays, the parts

department is set up as a separate profit center. Good parts managers can make more money than car salespeople, and the one at Don Massey caught on quickly to the profit potential of actively marketing cellular telephones to their customers."

Ken Dillon, Massey Cadillac's parts manager, embraced Palett's program without reservation. "Before we knew it, he became the top cellular car phone salesperson in any dealership in the country," Palett states. "He was selling 200 units a month—and this is the *parts* manager. Think of the potential the front-line salespeople were just ignoring." Tony Palett's own career was strengthened by his continued sales success. He rose to be Ameritech's top salesperson in his five-region area, and was number one among his peers selling in the automotive channel to Ford and GM dealers.

Passion and Persistence

Q.T. Keenan served as director of the cellular communications unit during much of Tony Palett's career with Ameritech and has managed numerous salespeople. "He's a pure, passionate seller," he says of Palett. "What sets him apart is that he loves the art of the chase as much as anyone I've ever coached. It's pure joy for him to wake up in the morning and say, 'I'm going after this piece of business.' He ties into that potential customer in ways that almost make him part of their team." Keenan adds that Tony identifies the hot buttons of his prospects and connects to what drives them. He does it so well that he consistently reaches 200 to 225 percent of his sales target, month after month after month.

Tony Palett would be embarrassed by such an appraisal of his selling abilities, yet humbled by its source. He was so relieved when Ameritech hired him, because he was—and remains—bullish about the future of the cellular telephone industry. His early ambitions at Ameritech were quite basic: to support his family and make a living, with the hopes of moving up the corporate ladder in the future. Those concerns are behind him today, and he says his goal now is to be number one every time. He believes his success is due to his being a very good reader of people and able to determine their needs, and having the ability to sense when to press forward and when not to.

> I believe that the key to sales success is persistence. I have a very, very competitive nature. I see other salespeople all the time and many of them just don't have that drive and motivation to always be ahead of the crowd. There is no perseverance to get the sale. With those barriers, they are

doomed to stay average sales reps, drifting along until they get fired. I love selling, and I strive for success in my field. I know my kids go to school and hear their friends say "My dad's an airline pilot," and "My dad's a neurosurgeon." Well, I consider myself on a par with any of them. Can they speak spontaneously before an audience of a hundred people? Can they sell an idea? I'm proud to be a salesman and I dedicate my success to my wife and kids.

Having observed the barriers that prevent other sales-people from becoming star performers, what impediments does Palett feel inhibit him from attaining even greater success? "I need to be a better listener," he admits. "I'm getting closer to that goal, but I recognize that I could be better yet. The other quality I'm striving to improve is to be more organized and methodical in my makeup. This is an area I want to enhance, and I'm working on it." This is typical of Tony Palett. He exudes confidence in his selling ability and product knowledge, yet has taken the time to be introspective. He has identified his own areas of weakness and is already taking steps to overcome them.

A superstar salesperson can identify with and relate to customers on different levels, and so it is with Tony Palett. From dealership owners to mid-level managers and floor salespeople, Tony has developed relationships of trust and mutual respect. "One of the things I like about Tony is that he sells to us on our level," said a salesperson at a Detroit Ford dealership. "He may be the top dog at Ameritech, but you'd never know it. When he comes in here, whether for a one-on-one meeting with me or to make a presentation to the entire sales staff, he comes across as Tony our buddy."

Palett considers Lee Iacocca—an icon in Detroit—to be the epitome of a good salesperson. "I think he was a marketing genius," he says. "He wasn't a bean counter. He created a need, inspired his employees and customers alike, and was a promoter. When he did those Chrysler commercials, he sold himself first, then his company. He looked you right in the eyes and said, 'You have my word on it.' *That's* a sales professional to me."

Dealing with Lost Sales and Delaying Tactics

So how does Tony Palett deal with the disappointments and lost sales opportunities that even superstars encounter? "As much as I love selling, I'll admit that sometimes it's hard to stay motivated out there," Palett admits. "If I lose a big sale that I've been working hard to get for a long time, it can get me down. My philosophy is that when life doesn't deliver what you've been counting on, just forget it and go on to the next one. It may be a hard loss to swallow, but you should never, ever, let a lost sale turn your attitude negative. You have to learn from it, and then go on. Never look back and whine."

Another problem that plagues salespeople is the prospect who continually puts the salesperson off. How does Tony handle these moving targets? "I cordially tell them, 'OK, I understand you cannot see me today. When can we get together? Is Tuesday good for you, or would Wednesday be better?' I try to pin them down, and one way to get a commitment for an appointment is to offer them a choice between two alternatives." He says that if you simply say "When can we meet?" it gives them too much latitude. They can tell you they're short staffed, or getting ready to do inventory, and tell you to come back in six months. By offering a choice—Tuesday or Wednesday? This week or next?—they will generally pick one of the choices he has given them. Either way, whether they choose A or B, he has won. He got the appointment.

The other type of customer that's difficult to tie down is the one who's very sweet and nice, but they never order. The sales rep calls on them time and again and they always say, "I'm sure I'm going to buy from you because I just love your product." Tony says that if month after month they never order, the salesperson has a problem. That sort of stall is one of the most difficult to overcome. The sales rep needs to discover whether it is just that person's personality to be nice to everyone. "You need to be straight with that type of person," he advises. "I say, 'That's fantastic! Then I'll get back to you in 30 days to confirm your order.' Then if there is no order forthcoming, I ask them directly, 'Are you sure you're not buying from somebody else?' At least then I've put him or her in a position to give me a definitive answer." Ultimately, if no business is forthcoming, Tony suggests that the salesperson should just drop the prospect and devote their time to calling on people who have real potential for giving them business.

Technology Creates New Opportunities

The future is bright for this young superstar. He still enjoys tinkering with inventions and has just applied for a patent on a revolutionary new type of cellular car telephone. This person with "the ability to know what will sell" is also expanding his product line with some exciting new technology.

> I was calling on a large car dealership that was undergoing extensive reconstruction. It was very difficult for them to communicate with their staff whenever they were away from their desks. The traditional method has been to use an outside paging system with noisy speakers all over the property. Whether you were in the service bay or the back car lot you would hear, 'Joe Smith, line four' incessantly, and Joe would have to interrupt his activity and find the nearest phone to pick up.
>
> I showed the dealer our new wireless PBX system. When an employee leaves their desk to go to a different part of the property, they take a small cellular phone with them. Any calls that come in to their desk telephone will automatically be rerouted to their pocket phone. It's efficient, it provides better customer service, and it eliminates the noise pollution from those outdoor paging systems which make the neighbors mad.

Tony has one of the $60,000 systems on customer trial already and hopes to install another one soon.

For all his enthusiasm over the modern technology he markets, Tony Palett is convinced that the secret to keeping customers satisfied is simple and old-fashioned. He says salespeople must listen to the customer's needs and then give them what they want. He points out that we are in a wireless communication world today, and with the proliferation of fax machines, cellular phones, and satellite technology, you might think that the need for face-to-face salesmanship is disappearing. Not so, Palett maintains. "You cannot establish rapport with a fax machine. You can't develop solid, long-lasting relationships using car phones. I predict that the need for customers and professional salespeople to meet face-to-face will increase in the future. It will be essential if the supplier wants to do a good job for long-lasting relationships."

Tony Palett has certainly been able to build those relationships. In the final research for this book, one salesperson said, "It's a great idea, and I think the stories will be inspirational to the readers. But most sales representatives might have difficulty identifying with the superstars who earn a million dollars a year and drive a Rolls Royce." If that is so, then Tony Palett is their type of sales superstar. He is the very best at what he does. He has been recognized by his peers, his company, and his customers as a motivated, knowledgeable professional. "He's one of the most aggressive people I've ever met—and I mean that only in the most positive sense," said Ken Dillon, parts manager at Dan Massey Cadillac. "Even when we're having a personal conversation, the subject always gets around to business. He's not even my rep anymore, yet he still calls me regularly. He's my idea man. The service from him is fantastic. It is above and beyond the norm of other sales reps. He is most definitely a real professional."

Tom Pappert

Chrysler's Big Man in Detroit

The Grand Ballroom of the Arlington Hyatt Regency, just outside Washington, D.C., suddenly grows quiet. Moments earlier, hundreds of Chrysler dealers had been engaged in numerous side conversations during the litany of corporate presenters. They now sit in hushed, revered silence as the keynote speaker is introduced. "Ladies and gentlemen, I give you *your* man at Chrysler, the guy whom every Chrysler dealer in America considers his friend—Tom Pappert." The applause is deafening. Many dealers stand. It is the welcome for a superstar who has risen through the ranks of corporate America from sales trainee to vice president of sales and service.

The Early Days

Like the opening of Dickens' *A Tale of Two Cities,* Tom Pappert's career at Chrysler could read, "It was the best of times, it was the worst of times." He has seen the number three U.S. automaker go from teetering on the brink of extinction to, barely a decade later, being celebrated as the quintessential corporate success, earning billions of dollars in profits. For Tom Pappert, today the top officer responsible for sales in the entire company, it has been a long and winding road to follow.

Tom Pappert's dad was a funeral director who also owned a Dodge dealership in Oakmont, Pennsylvania. Tom had helped on the car lot ever since he was a teen, so it was hardly surprising that he applied to Chrysler and joined the Dodge division right out of college in 1962. At that time there was a fairly long apprenticeship before salespeople were allowed to go out on the road to actually sell anything. Pappert began as a trainee, processing orders in the truck department. That job gave him a good background in product knowledge. He worked in the office for three years before ever calling on a dealer. When he did get on the road, he sold cars and all sizes of trucks for the Dodge division. Pappert says that those three years of inside training helped him tremendously when he began selling to dealers face-to-face. Not that he didn't make some mistakes. "I once put the wrong transmission in seven garbage trucks which the customer then refused to accept. Thankfully, Allison, the engine manufacturer, came to the rescue and modified the transmission in the field for me." At that time, Chrysler was producing twice the number of vehicles the dealers were ordering. Today, it is the reverse. He believes the training the salespeople receive in business management is better now than when he began.

Tom embarked on his career just weeks before the company dropped a bombshell and announced that it was canceling its entire DeSoto line. He still remembers the bad attitudes toward Chrysler as he ventured into the dealerships in his territory during the early days of his career. Tom Pappert admits that his was a different kind of selling than most people practice. After all, a Dodge dealer cannot decide to put in a showroom full of Chevrolets, and from whom else are they going to buy vehicles but from their Dodge rep? He explains that he is in a cyclical business, and he had joined the company just as one cycle started down. Then he noticed that the field salespeople who did the best were those who developed good relationships with the dealers. They all had very positive atti-

tudes and maintained a balance between the dealer and the factory.

Building Relationships of Trust

Pappert had 15 to 20 dealers in his territory, but the biggest part of his job was franchise development. Once the company identified an area where they felt they needed representation, he says he would knock on every door for 30 miles around. "Bear in mind that we were talking about needing a serious investment to open a dealership. A quarter of a million dollars, back in the mid-sixties, was the minimum required." After he had opened them up as a dealer, Tom made it a point to get to know their wife and family, and he saw his role as going far beyond being a salesman. He considered, himself their business partner, giving advice as a consultant on topics such as marketing, inventory management, and competitive advertising.

He looks at other Chrysler salespeople he has encountered over the years. Those who have progressed the fastest in their careers, he says, have also been the reps who developed trusting, friendly relationships with dealers. Those are the dealers who subsequently produced the most impressive results. "I have counseled salespeople and given advice to dealers. My experience shows that those who work hard to earn good dealer/rep relationships produce enormous benefits to both parties."

Pappert says he feels fortunate to have spent his whole career on the dealer side of the car business. "I represented Chrysler to the dealers, but the dealer has to also know that I represent their interests to the company," he explains. He believes that credibility is a major requirement. He had to prove to dealers that his handshake was worthwhile. Tom's relationships with his dealers paid dividends; the more he worked with them to develop strategies for them to sell more cars, the more his own sales increased. Chrysler noticed, and they promoted him often, dispatching him to parts of the country where they needed his talents: West Virginia, Pittsburgh, Florida, Kansas City, Chicago, San Francisco. By 1978, he had become general sales manager, just as the worst period in the company's history began.

Trouble in Motor City

Pappert recalls how dismal it was at Chrysler from 1979 to 1981. Yet even then, when he talked with dealers, he was straight with them. "I had built up an almost 20-year track record in customer relationships," he says. "What was I going to do, blow it all by being evasive when the going got rough?" For as long as he has been working in the industry, Pappert has told dealers that it is a cyclical business. He says it typically runs in five-year cycles. "No matter how good business gets, I tell my dealers, 'I hope you are taking some of this money you are making today and burying it in a coffee can, because I guarantee you're going to need it when the cycle swings down.'" After Lee Iacocca reorganized the company, Chrysler rebounded in 1982. Pappert believes that in the final analysis they strengthened the dealer relationships by the hard times they came through together.

An Honorable Man

Herb Yardley is the owner of Massey-Yardley Chrysler-Plymouth in Plantation, Florida, and has dealt with Tom Pappert for many years. "He does not fit the mold from which most salespeople are cast," he says. "He is reliable, consistent, and makes himself available to anybody. I could pick up the phone right now and get an appointment with him to discuss any problem. The worst thing that will happen is that at the end of the meeting, you might think, 'I didn't much like the s.o.b., but he treated me fairly.'" Yardley says that he once had a fleet customer dispute which the local Chrysler manager did not pursue for him because the manager was afraid of losing his job. The dealer took it to Tom and it was resolved immediately. "You can call 100 dealers and they'll say the same thing," he says. "You cannot do that with GM and Ford. Tom Pappert is an absolutely genuine, through-and-through honorable man."

The Executive Suite

In November 1981, Chrysler promoted Tom Pappert to the executive suite at their world headquarters, where he assumed the position of vice president of sales. In 1994, his responsibilities were further broadened when he moved up to vice president of sales and service, the position he currently holds. Despite the demands on such a senior executive, Pappert has never lost sight of the importance of maintaining personal relationships with the dealers. Every month he boards the company jet and visits dealers in 2 of the 25 zones around the country, updating them on industry trends and company developments, and listening to their concerns.

> I am not there to sell them anything. I'm there just to tell them what is on our mind and hear them tell us the same. They've got to know who you are and what you stand for. At the end of the day, your company is going to judge you on your productivity. However, the customer will base their decision on whether to give you future business on your relationship and reputation. That reputation is critical. It says who you are. That you are absolutely dependable, not from nine to five, but that 24 hours a day the customer can trust what you say. Contracts are things lawyers need, not salespeople. The other criterion for a good salesperson has to be a competitive spirit. People who don't want it [the order] enough, do not get it.

Pappert says his ambition when he joined Chrysler as a sales trainee more than 30 years ago was the same as all young executives: to conquer the world. Today, as the top sales executive during the period when the company has had the highest sales figures in its 70-year history, his goals have not changed much. "I want to be number one in as many things as I can," he answers. Some 400 salespeople ultimately report to Tom Pappert today. He believes the biggest reason for salespeople not making it now is attitude. He says he can talk with someone and know by the way they respond if their attitude is right. "You cannot just fly by the seat of your pants nowadays. I want to see someone with a real can-do attitude who really believes in themselves and their product and goes at it every single day. If you are the type of person who gets depressed after hearing three objections from the customer, you are in the wrong profession."

Demanding Excellence

Evidently, Tom Pappert is in the right profession. Back at the Arlington Hyatt Regency, 400 dealers from Chrysler's mid-Atlantic region are totally captivated by Pappert's presentation. "I'd give my right arm to be ambidextrous," he deadpans, using Yogi Berra's line. He addresses the fact that the dealers are selling cars faster than Chrysler can build them. "We're going to three nine-hour shifts to catch up." Then, once he knows he has everybody's attention, he switches gears and talks about the new culture at Chrysler.

> It is not about selling cars. It is about total customer satisfaction. Making nice is not the point of this presentation. I do not want to blow into town and lecture you. This is a togetherness thing. I promise you we will work on that together. But if you sell a customer a Chrysler car, the average dealer will make a profit of $7,363 over the length of that relationship. If you give such superlative service that your customer buys his future vehicles from you, your profit over that lifetime relationship averages $306,260. If you will join me in the pledge to deliver absolute, totally superb service to every customer who drives one of our cars out of your dealership, then I will promise you that every time you step up to bat, I will give you whatever it takes to hit one out of the ballpark.

Tom Pappert has spent an entire career developing relationships that were working partnerships. He has earned the high degree of trust the entire industry now has for him by showing that, in good times and bad, his word can be believed. From the reaction of the dealers in the room, and the record sales that Chrysler reported again for 1994, *this* batter is already on his way to the Hall of Fame.

Dyan Dobbyn

★

The Dynamic Dynamo
from D.C.

Dyan MacDonald Dobbyn is attracting attention from all over. Who is this superstar who entered the real estate profession less than a decade ago? What makes her so able to turn opportunities into sales successes? She does it not only in her own practice, but also for those sales agents who are fortunate enough to be accepted into the office she now manages. The story of the lady with the Midas touch has a most unusual beginning, yet one that illustrates that more than experience, education, and luck, the sheer will to win can conquer any challenge.

"In 1986, I worked for a commodity brokerage," Dobbyn recalls. "I liked the job well enough, and the hours were good for a working parent. Then we discovered that my husband had contracted cancer for the second time." As the mother of five young children, pregnant with her sixth, Dobbyn had to face the possibility of being the only source of support for a large family. She thought that a sales position, such as in real estate, might be the answer. "When I interviewed with several managers, I became profoundly depressed at the picture they painted of the real estate business," she says. "They told me that as a really good agent, I might make as much as $40,000, tops."

A Fast Start in a New Career

Nevertheless, she sat for her license and immediately began selling. Despite being in the late stages of her pregnancy, she shocked everyone at her agency by qualifying for the Million Dollar Sales Award and the Northern Virginia Association of Realtors Top Producer Award in her very first year in the business. She subsequently joined Long & Foster, one of the country's largest independent real estate chains. The next year and the one after that, Dyan Dobbyn continued to exceed the expectations of everybody except herself. How did this newcomer to the industry succeed where so many others fail? "I approached it as a business," she responds. "I knew where I wanted to be. I calculated how many transactions it would take to get me there, then I kept on prospecting until I achieved that level of success." As with so many other superstars, it all boils down to goal setting. After three years of successful sales, she set her eyes on managing an office, and she took and passed the broker's exam that is necessary for any office management role.

Long & Foster gave her an office to manage, and she was there for a year. "Then in April 1990," she says, "they asked me to open the new office in Alexandria, Virginia, which they call the Old Town branch. I set very clear goals. I told our CEO, Wes Foster, that I wanted to be Manager of the Year, and the top-selling office of any firm in the state of Virginia by my fifth year." She attained both goals in her third year at Old Town, and has been named Manager of the Year every year since. "Ambition is good," she declares, adding that you must not only have clear goals, you also need to set larger ones as you reach the small mileposts. "It gives you something to work for. Now my goal is to make this the highest-producing real estate office in the country." She gives herself two more years to get there, realizing that she is competing with companies in exclusive communities with very high average sales

prices. Although Alexandria has many upscale properties, the average sale price in Dobbyn's office is in the low $200,000 range.

Setting the Pace

For a person with no previous management experience, Dyan has set a remarkable pace at Long & Foster. Many real estate offices welcome any agent who wants to hang their license at the agency. The theory is that even if the agent is part-time to the extreme degree, *someone* they know will buy or sell a house each year and will let their friend handle it. Thus, an agency with a few dozen hung licenses might pick up several transactions each year that would otherwise be lost. Dyan sees it differently. "This is a full-time professional career for every agent I hire," she states. "I will have it no other way. When you work in my office, you will be committed to your clients, your career, and your profession."

She also has other ideas that contradict her industry conventions. Virtually every other real estate office in the country assigns its agents to answer the telephones. They call these three- or four-hour periods floor time, and any calls that come in from a potential buyer or seller become the lead of the floor-duty agent. In practice, the agent takes hundreds of calls for other agents or from other brokers for every genuine lead. Nonetheless, the commissioned sales agent saves the broker from having to pay a real receptionist. At Dobbyn's office there is no floor time. Professional receptionists answer the telephones seven days a week. Callers who respond to signs or advertisements are referred to the listing agent, who presumably knows more about the listing than anyone else.

Another tradition Dobbyn breaks is that of holding open houses. She explains that Realtors sell fewer than 1 percent of properties through open houses, and 10 percent of the buyers who walk in are sold other listings. "Why in the world would any client want unqualified members of the general public walking through their homes?" she asks. She feels it is a great disservice to ask her clients to vacate their homes for four hours so an agent can pick up business for other properties.

"My agents go out and find the business," she says. "They don't sit in somebody's living room waiting for it to come to them. Getting accepted in this office is very hard, and those few whom I do choose to join the team know that there will be no free ride. Everybody must pull their weight and maintain at least their proportionate share of the overall office goal as a minimum standard. Otherwise, they must leave. I just gave out nine notices this morning."

Setting Goals

Dyan takes a proactive stand in helping her salespeople realize their potential. Each of them, even the multimillion-dollar veteran producers, must have a business plan with clearly defined strategies for attaining their objectives. Every two weeks she meets with each agent to review their progress since the last meeting. She discusses their listing appointments, buyer interviews, and prospecting plans for the next two weeks. She asks each agent about their best accomplishment in the preceding fortnight and how they plan to get back on track if they have fallen behind on their annual goal. Dobbyn also holds a more detailed midyear review with each agent. At any one time, about one third of her salespeople are above their goals, a third are right on target, and a third of the agents were too optimistic in the figures they established. If she thinks the goals they are setting for the year are too high, Dobbyn tries to convince them to be a little more realistic. "I urge our people to set goals that are a stretch, but can be made," she says.

"I also let them know at the outset that I don't care how much business any one agent writes, there is no place here for prima donnas." Dobbyn reveals that there are some big producers in her area who would love to come to her office, but she won't touch them. "Production alone will not get you into this agency. I run this office, not the agents. I know that real estate agents are independent contractors, not employees *per se,* but when I say I want everyone to be at a sales meeting or to produce a written business plan, I mean everybody. If any agent wants to rebel against my policies, they are free to go be an independent contractor at somebody else's office."

The Dyan Dobbyn Difference

"There is a certain amount of jealousy about my agents and how productive they are," Dobbyn sighs. "I firmly believe that most real estate offices are run by non-producers or people who no longer have a strong emphasis on the importance of sales goals." Dyan Dobbyn's top agents seem to welcome her approach. They tell her that the more goal oriented she makes them, the better producers they become. She has one agent who was doing $2.2 million a year with her former company. The year after she joined Dyan's office, she did $7.9 million. "This year, she will sell more than $15 million, and do you know what her biggest beef was with her former agency? The manager would not take the time to sit with her to discuss her plans for reaching her goals." All she ever wanted was to be successful, and her manager was not interested in listening to, or helping, her.

Dyan talks about how she helps the Realtors in her office:

> I do one thing for my agents. I treat this like a business and show them, by example, that that is exactly what they should do, too. This is not a social meeting place for chat. This is not a little sideline to pick up some extra income when they can fit real estate into their schedule. I'll work with them to help set their business plan. They know they can count on me anytime to get them back on track, and if they need a mentor, they all know they can count on me. Despite space being at a premium here, I never ask anyone to share a desk. I wouldn't do that and I do not expect my agents to, either. I've had to terminate some salespeople for lack of production after they have been with the company a long time. But I have to be fair to everyone. No matter how much I like a person, they made a commitment to do certain numbers, and when they fail, they let the whole office down. I have had agents who, upon being terminated, have apologized for failing to live up to their promises. They are always welcome back if they get their act together.

The only time they don't get a second chance is for an ethics violation.

Sue Goodheart is one agent who joined Long & Foster's Old Town office in 1993 after interviewing with several other brokers in the area. Her first impression of Dyan was very favorable, and she says it has only gotten better. "She completely supports me as an individual and has helped me set, and reach, my goals every step of the way." In her first year in the business, Goodheart did $3 million in sales, then in 1994 it was $8 million. Her goal is to double that in 1995. "Dyan is right there to support you when you have doubts or get discouraged," she says. "Yet she never allows you to set yourself up to fall down. She makes sure that we work toward *attainable* targets and is there every step of the way to do whatever it takes to help me reach them. It is very exciting to be here in this office."

"We are very team oriented here," adds Dobbyn. "I am incredibly proud of this office and the agents who pull together to make it number one." Her office has developed a superb reputation, both within the community and throughout the Long & Foster chain. Dyan told the president, Wes Foster, that she was going to build what she had never found: an office whose manager sought to help the agents use more of their important selling skills by freeing them from the mundane chores. She now has a graphics designer to help agents with their marketing pieces, a processor, a receptionist, and office assistants. Walk around her office any time, any day, and you will notice only positive people. Agents often remark that they feel uplifted in this office.

This team spirit is not just the perception of management. It is evident as one observes salespeople dropping by the offices of their more experienced colleagues, seeking marketing advice, or just to try an idea on for size. Each of the top agents takes turns teaching new recruits their area of special strength. Although this is voluntary, Dyan says they are unanimous in their willingness to share their time and expertise with the industry newcomers. "The entire office is broken into groups, according to their production level," she says. "We have representatives from these groups on committees that consider training, advertising, community service, and office concerns. I believe we have the best ongoing training in the country right here in this office. We bring nationally known speakers in here. Charles Clark flew in from Florida to talk about personality selling, and we brought Mike Ferry in from California, too. The agents all share in the costs of engaging these speakers."

According to Dyan Dobbyn, the average Long & Foster sales agent sold eight transactions in 1993, averaging $162,114, for an annual income of $19,452. This is considerably above the national average of all real estate salespeople. Sixty-five percent of all Long & Foster agents sold less than $1 million. In contrast, Dyan's Old Town office had 51 Gold Team agents, each selling more than $3 million a year. Twenty-nine of her agents exceeded $5 million. Her top agent sold $14.8 million in 1993 and more than $17.5 million in 1994.

Overcoming Barriers and Burnout

Dyan believes lack of motivation is the biggest reason that perfectly capable salespeople do not reach their full potential. "I see so many people who consider themselves salespeople, but they have no goals, no burning desire to be successful," she says. "Some people—many people—are just not willing to do what is necessary to succeed." So what is her own barrier to greater success? "Time," she instantly responds. "But really, there is nothing keeping me from reaching my goals. Time is a perpetual challenge, but I have my plan worked out and I follow it every day. I will be there. This is one motivated lady. I have to be motivated," she adds, reading the interviewer's mind. "I have a rule that nobody in this office ever sees me down. I will not inflict myself on my agents that way. I owe it to them to always be up and motivated. If I'm feeling down, they will never know it. I was the same way with my customers."

Occasionally, a salesperson whose big one just got away seeks her counsel.

> My agents generally do not get upset over losing one deal. When someone confronts me who has let rejection or a lost sale get to them, I close the door and hold all my calls while we talk. If it is a big listing that they wanted, for example, I tell them, "You cannot lose something you never had. If you are working your business plan, one deal is not the end of the world." One of the first things I need to find out is if they have been sticking to their plan. I need to find out if they are so upset because they have not been working their plan and this was their only possibility they had in the pipeline. If so, I tell them, "Forget what happened the whole year up until now. Let's look forward. Your new plan starts right now. Let's walk back to the telemarketing room and work until we get an appointment." It is amazing how quickly a couple of new appointments will make you forget the last letdown.

Dobbyn also uses a strict work regimen as the antidote for salespeople who find themselves in a career rut. Even if it happens to an experienced agent, she asks them to meet with her privately at the beginning and end of every work day. She asks the salesperson to prepare a "perfect day plan," which describes how the best day imaginable would go for them. Then Dobbyn helps them work through a strategy to achieve it. "At 9:00 A.M. and 5:00 P.M. they must account for what they have done that very day to help meet the goals upon which we've mutually agreed. Working pulls people out of their depression in very short order," she says. "Accountability is the key to success in this business, yet I've seen managers let salespeople fall behind more and more, never making them accountable for their own success until it is too late."

A more likely scenario in an office filled with super-achievers is that an agent is so successful that they come perilously close to stress overload. Dyan Dobbyn has a plan for such situations. "I call them into my office and tell them what their colleagues and I have observed," she says. "Then I give them a choice: either get away and lay on a beach somewhere for a few days or give me their office keys right now and I will forbid them to come near the office for the same period. It saves them, and I have no problem being brutal with them on such matters, because I really care about my agents' welfare."

Someone once said, "You can get anything you want out of life, if you will just help others get what they want in life first." Dyan Dobbyn is the living testimony to that principle. Here is a mother of six young children who, in the late stages of pregnancy, qualified for the Million Dollar Sales club in her first months in a new career. This is a sales manager who talks the talk because she has walked the walk, setting sales standards few others have ever approached. A manager without a formal education, yet possessing management acumen for building and motivating others that few Ivy League MBAs can match. *This* is a fun office to watch hum along. This is a model for customer-driven excellence at the doorstep of the 21st century. This is a superstar's superstar, and her real estate office is about to hit the headlines as the top-selling one in the world. Stay tuned.

Putting It All Together

★

What you have just read is the string of pearls, the stories of 19 people who have earned the right to be called sales superstars. None of them reached their lofty pinnacles of success because they were the boss's son or daughter, nor did they attain such heights because of one big sale. Each of the people profiled has demonstrated their staying power by being at, or near, the top, year after year. Stephen Covey, nationally known speaker, management guru, and author of *The 7 Habits of Highly Effective People,* challenges us to "start with the end in mind" in our business and personal pursuits. As I interviewed these superstar candidates, and others who did not make the book, I never lost sight of Covey's admonition. I kept thinking about what the reader could learn from each candidate and the statements they made.

It is remarkable how these people of all ages, from vastly different backgrounds, industries, and geographic locations, have so much in common. The values shared by the top salespeople in America must surely be a valuable study for the reader who aspires to greatness in his or her field.

Their statements about the values they considered important were made without any reference to what previous candidates had said, but were remarkably similar to one another.

245

- They stress the importance of building relationships with the customer before ever trying to sell them anything.
- They focus on solving a customer's problems rather than selling a customer their product.
- They are described by the customer as non-aggressive, non-threatening, likable, and service-oriented. The customers genuinely enjoy the relationship.
- The salespeople are enthusiastic and love their jobs.
- Superstar salespeople see themselves as being self-employed. They believe their success is up to them, not someone else whom they see as responsible for feeding them sales leads.
- Without exception, they have a strong work ethic and understand that long hours are a permanent price they must pay for success.
- They are creative, flexible, and solution-oriented.
- Every superstar has written goals that they regularly check for progress.
- They are persistent without being annoying.
- They are always prepared when going before a customer.
- They acknowledge that they will not win every prospect, and instead of letting lost sales depress them, they learn from the loss and avoid repeating those mistakes.
- They are dependable and trustworthy.
- They are reluctant to be singled out for recognition, frequently pointing out that they are part of a team.
- They still derive enormous satisfaction from every sale, regardless of its monetary value to them.

Several of the sales superstars in this book are skilled in the following areas:

- Time management

- Personal marketing
- Niche selling or selling to a vertical special market
- Outstanding sales performance when confronted with the need to overcome hardships, illness, or pain

Two things rarely found in the candidates were:

- Bitterness or anger at lost sales
- Formal sales or sales management training

What an unremarkable list for such a group of over-achievers! There is nothing in those common traits that anybody with simple, basic intelligence does not already possess. So why are there so many mediocre salespeople and so few real superstars? Let's review some suggestions that the reader can implement tomorrow morning on your road to great achievement.

Taking Responsibility

Start with one fact. *You* are responsible for your own success. Not your company. Not your sales department. You. If you are blaming someone else for not generating enough sales leads for you to follow up, take ownership of the situation right now. You can decide to be the person sitting in the office waiting for the phone to ring, or you can be in control of your own future and get out and make it ring. Regardless of your product or service, you have to take charge of your destiny. It matters not that it is snowing outside today, or that your car is on the blink, or that you have a headache. Remember how Sid Friedman rejoices on blizzard days because all the mediocre sales-people have quit, and he has a city filled with prospects stuck at home next to the telephone. That changes the paradigm, doesn't it? Andrew Lanyi had never sold a thing in his life and did not even speak the language, yet he became the top salesperson in his company because he conceived of a creative plan to turn his weakness into strength. He spoke only Hungarian, so he looked up the telephone numbers of other Hungarians and made them his cold-call list. He turned lemons into lemonade and was soon drinking champagne. From Dyan Dobbyn, the mom pregnant with baby number six, to Irma Skaggs, who was forced to lay immobile in a full body cast for ten months, we have read example after inspirational example of salespeople who were given great reasons why they should not sell. Yet superstars never give in to adversity. They adopted the attitude so cleverly voiced by Sid Friedman, "If it is to be, it is up to me."

Ralph Waldo Emerson wrote, "A person becomes what he thinks about most of the time." Do you, like Chris Meunier, envision yourself as a top salesperson every day? Make the decision to jump-start your sales career today. Renowned management trainer Brian Tracy, author of *The Psychology of Selling*, warns, "Those who don't set goals are doomed to work for those who do." Write down your goal for where you will be in one year, then break your plan down into weekly increments so you can gauge your daily progress.

It is too bad that goal setting is not part of the curriculum at business schools, or even high schools, today. Legendary football coach Lou Holtz passes out cards to the high school seniors he wants to recruit. On one side is printed the Notre Dame team goals for that year. On the other is space for the student to list his top ten goals. "Sales is like football practice," says Holtz. "You've got to get out there again and again, even when you don't want to." Don't even try to set goals for yourself if you are in a company or industry you are not proud of. Quit. Go out and do something you enjoy. That is perhaps the first step to superstardom. There is not a person named in this book who does not absolutely love what they do.

Where to Find Customers

There is no way to cover every reader's industry here. Notice, however, that in this book there were two general ways in which the superstars found their clients. Those without a specialized niche tended to have strong marketing skills and invested heavily in getting their name and product or service out to their audience. Over 99.5 percent of the nation's Realtors probably think Ron Rush's telemarketing crew is an outlandish expense. Ron considers it a tremendous investment which has brought him hundreds of listings, buyers, and future leads.

Several superstars have identified a market niche and have turned their special knowledge of that vertical market's needs into a gold mine. Many of his competitors probably think Allan Domb is crazy for turning down expensive suburban listings. He is so crazy that he sold more real estate—$63 million—than anyone else in the United States last year, and every sale was in his special niche.

One other trait common to many of the superstars in this book is that at the conclusion of their business, they ask every customer to recommend a friend or business associate whom they feel could be a future client. Some, like Richard Kagan, rely on centers of influence for the bulk of their business, preferring to cultivate referral relationships rather than use traditional marketing techniques and cold calls. As Phyllis Wolborsky says, "The greatest compliment you could pay me would be to refer me to a friend." What a very logical and non-threatening statement from somebody with whom the client has just spoken every day for four or five months.

Serving the Customer

Whether they sell cars, copiers, or cosmetics, a common thread from every salesperson profiled was their emphasis on customer service. Not ordinary customer service, but superlative, outstanding service delivered quickly and consistently. How often have we heard rave reviews about a car salesman? Yet Marc McEver's customers effusively praise him, always talking about his outstanding service, integrity, and dependability first. In the confidential surveys which every car and truck buyer returns directly to Ford, his customers rated him in the very highest category of total customer satisfaction. Chris Meunier used her innate negotiating skills to design a mutually satisfactory solution to her client's overstock dilemma, Tom Pappert delivered the straight scoop to his dealers during Chrysler's darkest days, and David Koch took the initiative to drive a customer's package to New York. These are situations not taught in business school or Sales 101. They are core values that ring in a sales superstar's brain, saying, "Take care of the customer, and do it now." Remember Danielle Shepherd saying, "Selling has absolutely nothing to do with price, but everything to do with determining a client's needs and then providing solutions."

Take responsibility for your career and be creative and flexible in your approach to finding and serving customers. Be totally committed to delivering nothing less than superb, fast, consistent customer service. If you are able to do this with a degree of integrity that would make your parents and your children proud of you, you are well on your way to being sales superstars of the highest order. Good luck. Have fun!

Index

251